The Trauma
Mantras

II

Adrie Kusserow's *The Trauma Mantras* speaks directly to us. This is a testament of reckoning, a solid collection of distilled observations, an upturning of physical and psychic realities, as well as heartfelt reflections. This poet's hard work goes to the pay dirt of realism wherever the speaker travels. These poetic prose pieces are well-made actions—not merely generated but lived—with jagged edges. And the reader must be ready to go there, to feel and dream the rhythmic burn of language as rage and beauty converge, and to arrive at a place of needful contemplation. The speaker faces a revealing juncture: "Our hunter-gatherer bodies are still designed to vibrate when close to another's animacy, the frenetic hum and bubbling of the urge to describe a tulip, peach, wild rose, mountain, or fox before the next text comes in." It is this desire to venture into the pulsating clay, even to the other side, that requires a give-and-take, but not by a typical directive or calming image map. *The Trauma Mantras* is exciting, and perhaps this is more so because the speaker raises questions as a tool or weapon. Not for the sake of anecdotes, but for how one might journey to truly feel, to learn, to be(come) part of personal inquiry with eyes on the collective. In this sense, each piece is a deep voyage. We readers engage multiple voices revealing personal histories of hurt and pain, reaching out for vital connections and mature insight—hurting for what we risk being made of. The voices this writer gives us are a treasure because of the intrinsic dialogue of contrasts. Going through dilemma and pain, coming to a curative pause, and then we realize ascension most likely is a long road ahead.

As an anthropologist and a poet, Kusserow is also a serious teacher and activist, someone whose commitment runs deep. Her passion is here in each piece. And she does not let herself off the hook as she delves into numerous social and political ills troubling humanity. In this sense, hers is a world voice. The reader cannot escape understanding the poetry on every page of *The Trauma Mantras*. It reveals but does not blame. Yet what we witness through imagery becomes evidence—woven in the language. And in this breathing music we hold ourselves accountable. We feel these pieces, even in those moments when we're caught slightly off guard.

The Trauma Mantras is a gift across cultures. And it is only natural that vicissitude is casted in our journey. The word groupings throughout the text, for the most part, slow the reader until they grow momentarily engaged in meditation. Yes, Kusserow is an anthropologist and a poet, and we must hear and feel both fused as one—an immersion—tonally. Each focus reveals art. Such brave work exposes any unearned grace note; this poet gives the world a robust spirit of truth-seeking. Her language is straightforward, caring, and gutsy. What more do we dare ask an artist-seer to surrender or give of herself?

The Trauma
Mantras

Trauma is cloudy, not solid like measles . . .

CAROLINE MOOREHEAD, *Human Cargo: A Journey among Refugees*

Meena encouraged Manju to express the worst of her thoughts. It was said to be the modern, healthy way of coping.

KATHERINE BOO, *Behind the Beautiful Forevers*

The Trouble with Stories

Indian Brothel Raid

DARJEELING, WEST BENGAL, INDIA

This is a story of a story I wanted to be the hero of, but wasn't. I wanted to tell it over and over, propping it up on prominent display back in the great USA, until I rose like an angel from my perpetual shame. What shame? That's another story, suffice it to say I was desperate. How I imagined being part of those raids, rescuing the kidnapped girls, but I'd only raise suspicion in a brothel. So instead a Nepali man from our NGO visited the brothel for months, pretending to be a customer, finally gaining Smriti's trust, the date of the raid was finally set. I was to be nowhere near the premises.

After a raid, most of the girls don't want to talk to anyone, but Smriti finally agreed to come to our office way up high, above the grimy taxi station, above the chaos of bodies, honking horns, and petrol fumes, a dumpy room with chipped brown plastic floors, a cracked window, where everyone shivered, drank Nescafé, and wore down coats all day.

She arrived dressed up, made up, as if auditioning. You could tell that someone had gotten to her, maybe from the Swiss NGO down the street, convincing her that telling her story over and over to a stranger would lighten her mind, release her trauma, help her sleep, make her feel less polluted.

As Smriti spoke, I tried not to reimagine my own grand rescue narrative. (Imagine the shame of my own ego poking up through the landscape of *her* suffering.) I lay low, as small as could be, accepting the story she'd boxed up so neatly for me, and trying to just sit in her presence.

Finally, I asked her, How did they not find you in the first raid?

They make us hide in tunnels, behind trap doors, in bunkers, attic cells, and blackness.

You can make yourself so very small if you try. You fold into yourself, become darkness, until there's nothing but breath.

On my walk home that day, I expected the story of me the great raid redeemer to rise up, hissing its victory song. It's amazing how long it takes some stories to wear themselves out of the mind. But Smriti's story silenced mine. Sometimes others' stories multiply your own, sometimes they cancel each other out. Sometimes one story puts another into relief, exposing the cheesy Bollywood drama that it is. As for Smriti, who knows if telling her story actually helped like our NGO told her it would. If she limped back to her village lighter, or heavier, I'll never know.

The Sweaty Tribe

DAYA DAN ORPHANAGE, MISSIONARIES
OF CHARITY, KOLKATA, INDIA

Calcutta becomes the Disneyland of suffering.
—McKenzie Wark

Here comes another white girl in hip-hop, dreads, tattooed in Buddha, Krishna, Shantideva, her body a road map of past religious Kwik Stops. You can smell them, all patchouli and caged nerves, ponytailed and sandaled, toting their ratty knapsacks, grungy journals, emerging from the taxis, bone-tired, hauling their boulders of guilt up the crumbling stairs, their tiny portable traumas. Winding their capes of doubt through the muggy faiths of others, stumbling up the steps, repentant.

And I have to love them, because I am no better, though sometimes I think I am, sitting on the stairs on my lunch break, watching them arrive.

Months pass, even after the monsoon takes its heavy skirts elsewhere, still they come, dogged through the swollen heat, their sticky, discontented moods, tall blonde hungry ghosts, padding after the nuns, sheepish and sweaty.

That I am part of this sweaty tribe I have to admit. Over and over I baptize myself, bending into the bodies that litter the cribs, wincing at the small, clingy deaths in midstream, rising up with another twisting, sticky child, kneading the gnarled bodies that refuse to flatten, muscles stiff as pipe.

At Daya Dan, we are all addicts now, to the ecstasy of being humble, of being no one, of bowing our heads. So very tired of our righteous, lonely theologies. All of us dunking ourselves in India's dying, coming up for air, dunking again, the toddlers turning toward us, whole fields restless and rebellious for touch.

Mary, the oldest orphan, still here after all these years, sitting like a queen, perusing her kingdom of cribs, holding court with her sweat-drenched devotees. They found her at Howra train station, dragging her legless torso on the *Calcutta Times*, limping monkey trailing behind her. On hot days, we gently hose her down, avoiding the leaking plum where pigeons made a meal of her eye.

This is how it goes at Daya Dan, the nuns starched stiff with Christ, tying a defiant toddler to a crib, barking their orders to the wet-eyed overwhelmed Westerners. And I have to love them, the wet-eyed ones, because I am no better, though sometimes I think I am.

Revised *Lonely Planet Guide to Holy Men*

DELHI, INDIA, AND DHARAMSALA, INDIA
(HOME OF THE TIBETAN GOVERNMENT IN EXILE)

I was nineteen when I asked the dashing Tibetan man at the Dharma Tours travel shop how to get to Dharamsala, where the Dalai Lama lived. His long black hair glistened like a river. It was the dozens of prayer flags hanging from its storefront, the Tibetan incense wafting from under the door, that lured me in. I thought I smelled yak wool, salt butter tea. Like many upper-middle-class Americans tired of my kind, I was after some Buddhist authenticity.

My loose brown hair was streaked with the powdered pinks, yellows, reds, and blues of Holi, which was joyously rioting through town. I looked like a Deadhead, streaked with color. He knew my type, told me his mother was from the United States, then shut the door, locked it, and asked me to marry him.

When I said *No, thank you*, he cocked his head and smiled, then laughed, telling me how brave I was, traveling alone. I knew right then I'd be punished. And I was. I never got to the bus station. Instead, he dropped me in a slum of riots, tear gas, fires, and men throwing glass bottles. They were using the chaos of Holi to kick some Muslim ass. Across the street, one blue modern bus stood like a glistening whale shifting and heaving. *Get out*, he said.

I knocked on the bus door, the gills wheezed open. Aisles of male Sikhs headed toward the Punjab, one preppy Western man in a button-down shirt, an architect from Boston. Silly me, I sat near him for protection (West against East), until 2 a.m., when his hand crept up my thigh, his tongue like a clumsy eel in my ear. When I told the bus driver to stop, he gave me his crumbled biscuits warm from his pocket before releasing me into the cold night.

Into nothing but an empty dirt road, except for one rickshaw driver, half asleep, who wakes and stares, until I show him some money, and he mounts his bike, his back rippling with shadows and snakes as he strains over the potholes. He keeps looking back at me, as if he's captured a witch, and he'll get in trouble for this.

Finally he stops at the town bus station, an empty room with neon lights, flies, biscuit wrappers, and one long steel table. Six young men paw my hair while they giggle, intrigued by my blue plastic hair clip. They were boyish and innocent, gentle and kind, teasing each other. So I stood for them like a mannequin as they turned me around. They only wanted to inspect this lone female alien and the contents of her bag. So I emptied my purse on the table and excitedly they combed through it until dawn eked through the dirty windows.

This is what they don't tell you about the Punjab in the *Lonely Planet*, that they waved and cheered like soccer moms as I boarded my last bus, my pockets stuffed with their wives' spiced paratha.

In Dharamsala, more men, monks mostly, whose bulbous egos had definitely not dissipated like fog. Because they spoke English, I hung out with the Western monks, most of them runaways from wealth and chalky white Gods that had only punished them. They brought no comfort to the emptiness (*sunyata*) I was trying to practice, the strict meditation I had come to hate. Like them, maybe I was using my practice to kick some Protestant ass. How they loved to snicker and giggle at my confusion, pretending it was enlightened laughter. I was so lonely I would have taken anything pure or kind from them, but nothing was offered except a subtle mockery and more beers. Not one of them ever touched me, but I still wince from the belittlement they doled out, calling it *crazy wisdom*.

You see, the *Lonely Planet* doesn't tell you that under the guise of Buddhism many evil things lurk. That in Shangri La, you have to be careful which men you go to for help, because not all of them are what they seem, especially the Western ones who wait for you to come knocking on their door, crouched like wolves under the hoods of their little red monk robes, their teeth glistening as you walk in and tell them you just want to learn about the Dharma.

Patchwork Quilt for a Congolese Refugee

WINOOSKI, VERMONT

Not all want to relive the experience, rather they need help building up structures
that contain and imprison it. Then they need to learn to live, and move on.
—Aida Alayarian, Refugee Therapy Center

None of the white coats predicted the autumn leaves would be such a trigger.
Every fall she grew suspicious as the days passed, sly and dark, behind her and
the earth shifted slowly in its seat. Blood orange blotches caught and spread
like birthmarks along the Green mountain range. In the cold, balding woods
where they told her to walk, for exposure, she could hardly breathe when she
saw it, the sugar maples' gory neon spill, as if kicked in the gut, the first burn-
ing blood veins, scarlet bolt of lightning.

✦

Week after week of exposure, she did not improve.

This is what I told her:

She could sit quietly, letting the lonely Catholic priests sew the dull needle
of Jesus through the little jungle brute who crammed a gun up her nose. She
could spend her whole life picking through images of gang-raped, machete-
gutted women, cobbling together a patchwork quilt with its bold "African"
traumas in vogue now. She could fall in love, with a rapt audience clinging to

her words as she TED-talks the noble tragedy of her story. She could drag her past around like the American kids with their baby blankets, demanding their rights to bedtime stories. She could even sell it at boutiques where Americans shop for Fair Trade.

Or, as the eerie geese fly south above her and the cold creeps across her skin, as crimson gashes rip through the hills with their brilliant mad infections, she could let the blood leaves break her apart, let go of it all, and finally just begin.

Trigger Fields

YEI, SOUTH SUDAN, AND COLCHESTER, VERMONT

In the postapocalyptic landscape of South Sudan, I'd stick to the main road, anywhere else was pockmarked with bombs. Clunky Mine Action vans raced around like insects with beeping antennae and gangly prods, men dressed like astronauts.

Cattle herders, farmers. Children digging for termites, intrigued by the toy-like objects in the dirt, mothers looking for firewood or food. None of them could read posted warnings.

We faculty at the college in Vermont where I teach, we are slowly learning to read the warning signs settled on our students' bodies. We are adjusting accordingly. We are walking the main road more and more.

This morning a student tells me she is too triggered by my assignment to talk to someone about death, that it could also trigger the person she is interviewing, which could cause suicidal ideation. Another says the article on eating disorders was too triggering to read, so could she be excused from the quiz? Another no longer trusts my colleague enough to do the assignments, because twice he used the wrong pronouns and she no longer feels safe in class.

Triggers, triggers everywhere.

In class I begin to doubt myself.

My biggest fear, a Tourettesian explosion of unwoke words I never intended, so I opt for humor, lightness, I tread softly, I stay on the main road. I reconsider the child marriage film I was going to show.

Later I visit my Sudanese friend Ayen in the hospital. I knew her aunt had been missing. They found her hanging dead from a tree, a suicide. Ayen lies listless in the hospital bed. Ever since, she's started waking in the night, half her body paralyzed, the left side of her body numb, like cold chicken. Then the other. There's no predicting its logic.

The white coats have run every test possible. *No medical reason for this*, they say, masking frustration. (Her affect is flat, which further frustrates them, as if they hope the distress will at least manifest in some form of facial angst.)

I tell them she went into a coma after her mother died, that not all cultures process distress psychologically. I sense their pity, as if she is developmentally delayed in the trauma world and someday will present this psychologically, the true home of all distress.

Three hours later, their pity still hovers, poor Ayen, she isn't quite up to speed in the prized mental health literacy that spreads like wildfire around the globe.

They label it *conversion disorder*, because what "should" be manifested as psychic trauma is presenting somatically.

I hate the mind/body dichotomy, but in this instance, on this hospital floor with its screaming fluorescent lights punishing us all, there's no other verbal place to go, so I corral myself into one or the other as I talk to the doctor.

Meanwhile, a snake in my mind doubts and uncoils. So what if trauma slides underneath Sigmund Freud's gaze, and slithers out, never manifesting as psychological pain? Why do we insist it parade in the psyche in order to be legit?

The trouble with trauma is that it has never heard of René Descartes and it only came into being at the end of the nineteenth century. In countries far from here it moves below the psyche, slippery as a fish, all over the body, numbness here, paralysis there. Prefers the space of soma to the cramped quarters of psyche.

While in the hospital, I tell Ayen there is no medical reason for her shifting paralysis, I hint at the possibility that this might be linked to her aunt's suicide, but I can tell there's no buy-in.

Two days later she is out of the hospital, lipstick on, tie-dye dress, posting her usual Dinka dance routines on Instagram with glitter sparkle filter. We shop at T.J. Maxx. I ask her husband how she explains the paralysis.

Just a bodily fluke that has left her now.

So trauma slipped in and out without her psyche ever suffering. I feel cheated, then ashamed for feeling cheated. Behold the residue of the Protestant work ethic where we have to work for, suffer with, our trauma, don't we? Isn't torment one of my most common rites of passage? I envy her. Distress too started in my body, but the psychogods of New England swept in like an owl and clawed it up in great tufts, bringing it back up to the psyche to nest. From here on out it needed aggressive self-work, medication, monitoring, in order to lessen.

When America falls in love with a mental illness, it falls hard. Its devotion primal. It sees nothing else. It runs amok, full-on Freud. It wants what it wants. It celebrates its noble cause of defending the traumatized at any cost. It herds them into safe zones, says, *There, there.*

It's so busy triaging the individual, the collective gets forgotten (mundane rampant poverty and inequality lack the same clout). Stress, confusion, aging, loneliness, sadness have none of the unassailable moral high ground.

I look out on this class of sleepy students. Be compassionate, I say to myself, they've simply fallen in love. Suddenly I picture them, a field of owls, suspicious yellow eyes on full alert, clutching their tufts with their talons, guarding them with their whole college life. They are just learning how to do this, a bit clumsy, forgetting at times to maintain their rage long enough to show up for one-on-one meetings, tufts of triggers in their teeth and claws, threatening to bite anyone who tries to rip them away. In the great swampy suffering symptom pool of American college life, you turn to the stories that get you help—the ones with bold colors, exotic plumage. Loneliness, sorrow, malaise, meaninglessness can't compete.

At the beginning of class I told them this was a class on refugees, I thought I had warned them, but you can never be too careful. So today I throw them bits of meat from my bag, today I make them happy, I want no trouble. A little bit of YouTube here, a docile excerpt from the *New York Times* there, even an SNL skit for good measure. I even let them keep their hats on, low around the eyes, like the hooded trainers of falcons, minimizing negative stimuli, calming them, gradually getting them used to the worlds they fear will destroy them.

Quarantine Dreams

UNDERHILL, VERMONT, AND DHARAMSALA, INDIA
(HOME OF THE TIBETAN GOVERNMENT IN EXILE)

All day long I watch the snow fall, the single crow on its perch the only punctuation mark I've heard all day. Across the field, a fox pounces for a mole as if in a cartoon, and my heart is buoyant as I watch it flip and flop, hurl itself nose first.

Downstairs my son is trying to find a tune on the piano. I can tell he's riding the notes, without trying to control them. Something is flowing through him that is not entirely himself. I can tell when he's quieted his mind enough to follow the pull of something larger, like a tug from a line deep underwater. From my bed, my antennae prick up, the hair on my arms is the first to sense another presence. The notes rise up through the ceiling and soothe.

Day five of quarantine, someone told me to analyze my dreams, that quarantine dreams are the stuff of buried trauma, but I refuse to mop them up with pop psychology, put them in the tiny stuffed cages of the American Traumasphere. They comfort me in the way they leak into the morning, seeming to come from everywhere but me. What a shame if they arise merely from the individual body, the stuffy therapist's den. How lonely that would be.

Maybe in sleep, with the mind's government soldiers off duty, the non-human, the shadows, the collective past floats in, if we're lucky.

I let myself sleep. And in between I let memories gather until enough of them form a plot I recognize. I'm careful, I don't go after them too hard, I don't want to scare them away.

My first trip to Dharamsala, there was no dream, only the fog moving in while trekking toward the pass, until I couldn't see the yaks five feet away, or the yellow beaks of rhododendron pushing up through the snow. Once again I had strayed off the path and my group would be pissed. Lost, I slept in a dilapidated retreat hut, small as a doll's house, the rats crawling over my zipped-up sleeping bag until I punched them off like potatoes with my fists.

The next morning the caretaker monk with the scarred cheek told me he had a dream I would visit him, but I knew I was just lost. Perhaps the monk was using the dream to make me stay. I had been told not to trust any men, even monks. I had never thought of dreams as that solid before, raised in a place where the hierarchy of reality is based on materiality. I could tell for him the dream was as real as wood or stone. So I considered committing to the weight of it, let it pin me like a paperweight on my flighty self and stayed an extra day.

In the evening, he brought me salt butter tea, started rhythmically slapping his hands, his eyes glistening fiercely, breaking me into what he called the *luminous ice of unknowing*. I was hungry and cold. Every time he slapped, I winced from his shock therapy. He kept telling me the slapping would wake me up from my dream. At least that's how I remember it now, but it's hard to keep the past from wriggling out from under the present's hungry gaze, using it for its own purposes.

Smiling the entire time, he told me how he'd fled from Tibet after the torture, his long, frostbitten journey. How resilient, I thought, picturing the hardiness of physical material, picking up a stone to symbolize. I let the stone drop into his hand. *No, no, sems pa chen po*, he said, pointing to the sky. Resilience was fluid, not solid, spacious, humble, flowing like water over rocks, a gentle expanding compassion, rather than a stiff bouncing back, or a thickening of borders of the self. He giggled. Resilience was not a Marlboro Man with a stern jaw, but a vast and spacious mind that did not individualize suffering. *Sems pa chen po*. How strange, I thought, not to personalize trauma. But I liked this place, this new place where nothing, not even suffering, was really mine anymore.

I learned in Buddhism, when you reach a place where the world seems fluid, like a dream, something you can swirl your fingers through, so little inherent substance to anything, it's a good thing. Like finger painting, you revel in the colors and textures, bold glops and streaks, the pungent smells like giant moist paws, the giddiness of freedom, all of this merging and swirling, all of this, before the canvas dries, and we're trapped.

Getting the Story Just Right

WILLISTON, VERMONT
(SUDANESE REFUGEE HOME VISIT)

Sitting with the girls and Ayen underneath the squawk of their giant television, whose neon colors bathe and swallow our faces as I prattle on about my day. The girls cuddle up beside me on the brown Salvation Army couch with its blue embroidered Dinka doilies. I ask about Ayen's health since her recent hospitalization for paralysis.

Four checkups later, I can tell she's practicing a new story, like she's trying on a glitzy American dress and she isn't sure if it fits her or if she can carry it off. I can even tell she's tried the word on her own, in front of the mirror, to get it just right. *I had some stress, too much stresses,* she says in her clipped Dinka accent. I respond with the most neutral facial affect I can muster, she tells me, *Doctors say no stress, stress is bad,* and with this, I admit my heart sinks, I can see she's taken up a story that blames herself, her lifestyle, for the unexplainable paralysis, instead of the global plights of refugees.

I've seen this before, refugees reaching for sanctioned American stories around suffering, trying to stuff themselves in. Desperately grafting themselves onto the trunk of the most popular legitimate story about suffering in this liberal town, then praying that it takes, waiting for their vines to grow upward and curl around. Usually, this involves moving toward a more singular, psychological view of the world and themselves. What withers in America are the clumsy, folksy, smelly stories that smack of soul, spirit, ancestors, cows, witches, tribe, too much history.

We like our stories shiny, sharp, to the point, dazzling, direct, like a well-trained TEDx talk.

Sometimes the two become one, the refugee and the story in vogue.

I wonder how thoroughly Ayen will come to inhabit the story of *stress*. At that point, who am I to challenge it, and coach her into something more *authentic* when it's settled deep in her veins, deep as bone into her own body?

I resent how the doctors gave her a story because they couldn't tolerate no story at all.

Yesterday I felt a Somali woman waiting anxiously to try a new story out. Gumming the story inside her, waiting patiently for me to finish mine, trying to hide her impatience, oh the joy of letting it first flower from her lips, this new script with its promise of freedom, at first limping then rippling across the table where we share tea and biscuits.

She was presenting me a gift of sorts, proof that she was adapting to life here.

You can't blame humans for wanting stories that come with a warranty, a community, a medical insurance sanction, a friend, a club, a membership, a college degree. Stories wither in isolation, feed and shape the depths of us most when nurtured by the village.

In America, we love individualism, a story that has a hero who stuck up for their rights, persevered. Asylum seekers bend their stories in the way they think will most convince the interviewer, sometimes downplaying their torture in favor of a more gripping, rugged, heroic American plot. They learn to tell a story that begins with "I" instead of "Long ago" or "My tribe" or "In the beginning, there was creation . . ." They learn history and context must be sloughed off in favor of the unique idiosyncrasies of the single "I"—or else the interviewer grows bored or, worse, suspicious.

After my visit with Ayen and the girls, I walk back out to my car, buzzing with stories about our encounter that I already want to tell others, stories that prove I'm an anthropologist, that give me academic street cred. Versions of stories rehearsing themselves around my mind, which has yet to let one settle as its prize. I will tell these stories from the field to my students, and they will digest them, consume them, not in all their anthropological complexity, but as a badge of my anthropological honor, that I am out there in the trenches with humans different from themselves. This is what they paid for, to hear from people such as myself, to tempt them with stories that make their heads rise up off their phones.

But this is not the story I want them to leave class with.

I remember my mother saying, *Choose your story well.* Once I coax one into being and let it graft onto my mind, it might be hard to remove later, *without cutting down the whole tree*, she'd say.

What I wish my mother had also told me was, *Try not to faint from dizziness, dear, as there are so many stories to choose from.* Stories spin off from the internet, on the sides of buses, billboards, at churches and mosques, from the mouths of coaches, teachers, therapists, caseworkers, and employers.

No one ever said it would be easy, getting the story just right, especially the stories that shape the core of who we are, moving the cells of our body in whole flocks and murmurations, shifting, binding, freeing, and trapping.

Calla Lily, Condom

KAMPALA, UGANDA   *For Willem, age 3*

Told not to, I went to the bus station anyway, to pay my translator, the one who'd fought in the Red Army as a child. He was prone to anger, I didn't want him to explode.

It was getting dark. Of course we got lost, so I held you tight, the drunks pawing me as I wove through the stalls sticky with beer and urine.

I don't know if you knew it, but we were winding through alleys where dogs bled from their butts, a freshly pummeled woman lay like pounded meat in the gutter, reeling from the punches for requesting a condom, or if you heard the gurgle that was blood in her cheek as she slumped into a puddle while the drunken crowd jeered.

Or if you smelled the acrid fumes rising from a pile of sleepy boys sprawled across each other like a litter of puppies, nursing jars of glue.

Swollen broken nests of those slums, I could hardly breathe but for the rotting and the birthing.

You started to chatter, I said, *Hush, sweet boy, hush*.

Finally a man offered us a taxi in exchange for helping him with a visa. Of course I said yes, I said yes way too many times.

Back at the Lake Victoria hotel, the hibiscus lashed its red tongue into the cool night, as wealthy *muzungus** spread their stiff white napkins starched and white as calla lilies across their laps.

Cooing, clueless, you could hardly see the difference between the squashed condom the man threw at her in disgust and the crushed lily flattened by the *muzungu*'s high heel, between the bleeding, the bleeding from everywhere there was an opening, and the languid arch of the red hibiscus sprawled against the night.

* *Muzungu* means "white person" in East Africa.

Western Psychonauts of the Postpartum Period

BURLINGTON, VERMONT

In the end, I only have what slips through my fingers, the stuff of dreams, fading. My feverish brain drugged up and loopy, held together only by flashbacks, of a pelvis cracking open, all fissures and splits. I couldn't sleep in case the contractions exploded, even though my child slept beside me. The birth was all done, over, my brain on high alert, watching for more danger.

No rest, only the bits of panic jumping off the hot skillet of my brain. An exquisite manic madness, agile, deft, quick.

I wake and dip, wake and dip, surfacing under the moonglow of a large black TV, alien mother of this ward, spewing silent colors that splash and swallow. Gloved mummies come and go, pressing my uterus for leftover blood.

I didn't opt for a lotus birth, carrying the placenta around in a bowl, still attached to the baby, salting it for freshness, waiting for the umbilical cord to fall off like an old withered bean. I wasn't among those in my yoga class that viewed the cutting of the cord as traumatic, unnatural. To me this was just more hegemonic spread of *Trauma, Inc.* way up into the birth canal. My newborn was fine, it was my brain that was on fire.

Over and over nurses asked, *How are you* feeling? I resist the generic and dopey feeling words at my disposal. Metaphor's much better, but what nurse has time for that? Every hour or so, a peasant woman with large muscular hands washes my soggy heart in a stream, twisting, wringing, kneading it into a primal ache that has no name.

When my daughter cries, it startles the billion pigeons of my cells, takes forever for them to settle down and stop clucking. But they do, sometimes enough for whole caves of awe to hollow me out as I finger her pink toes, small as corn niblets, ears covered with fiddlehead down.

When she was satiated, the white pearl of milk slipping from her mouth, the startle of twitches, smiles, pouts, jerks, began, the stuff American adults like to make meaning out of, psychological meaning, that is, like, Oh she's a happy child, stubborn or determined.

I tell my students we *Psychopomorphize* the twitching blob in the crib, and play pin the tail on the donkey with Freud. And thus begins our descent into the Psychologized Self, where a gas bubble crowning from a "grin" means she's confident, happy, when just as easily we could have spoken of spirits, clouds, dreams, the moon, creation myths, the mycelial web's magnetic pull, or nothing at all.

For comfort I reached out to other new mothers, over the phone. For days, I wandered into the dark pools of their depressions and emerged lonelier than before. We were all becoming Psychonauts, exploring, but stranded, washing up on the shores of the Island of Psyche over and over. Never have I been so lonely as I was in the land of Postpartum Depression, with its reigning Queen of Hormones and the Princess Serotonin. The narrative I was given smacked of a first-grade reader. The Queen of Hormones was whacked out, unreliable, in the wrong place at the wrong time. Cross-eyed, disheveled, a nut job, she was not to be trusted. The Princess Serotonin was apparently anorexic and in scarce supply. And then the boring King, with his same old story of father loss and fear of abandonment, which he belched out proudly between burps.

I remember my fieldwork in New York City, the Haitian nannies on Park Avenue, taking the white infants out to the park while their cachectic blonde mothers ran on the treadmill. How they'd laugh and mimic the neurotic mothers hunched over their infant's crib, the fretting and turbulent weather of the upper-middle-class skies above them.

But I feel for these mothers. In the land of Park Avenue parenting, child development doesn't just happen without prodding, stimulation, and immense parental angst. Ever since *parenting* became a verb, it's these women who ultramarathon. I remind myself, it's also these women we owe utmost tenderness and compassion, just as we would any other exotic tribe. After laughing with the nannies in the hope that this will build rapport, I feel cheap and mean. I should know better.

Sometimes I can sound lofty, anthropological, as if I'm high up in the sky again, looking down on humans fumbling around. Though I love it up here, of course I'm no different, I haven't escaped *Project Individual Self*, locked as I am in the plush royal velvet of my exquisite emotions, whose ornate rooms and neuroses I have explored and analyzed and mostly made my home since childhood.

But lately something else is going on. Lately, even when I try, I cannot stuff my experience into psychologized systems of thought, I let them stay outside, and when they howl, and want a label, I listen, but I don't let them into the therapist's den, or the DSM, because they are wider and wilder than that, because don't you think this is the least we can do, we humans, let ourselves be processed, held, understood by more than just us?

Years later, when a beautiful pregnant colleague wants postpartum advice, I retreat into Hormones and Serotonin talk, because I want to give her something resembling advice, warmth, solidarity, an elder passing on wisdom. So I chatter, I watch myself from above actively reinforcing the biomedical discourse I just critiqued in class.

It's what we do as humans when we want to connect, we turn to what's available, we hope it will do the trick, we string tired word stitched to tired word between us, in rituals of rough encapsulation and domestication, and sometimes it has to be enough, this noble kind of reaching, a dogged, clumsy kind of loving, weaving our coarse nets between us, pulling each other ashore.

Refugee Christmas Eve

NORTHEAST KINGDOM, VERMONT

Hush, remember, the wind was howling, snow squalling into eddies and currents that writhed across the fields, vanished into blackness. I was sitting by your side, on the locked "low-stim" floor, as you sat, stunned, regal Dinka of the Blue Nile, on the psych ward's stiff white sheets, like a fallen blackbird beating against the glass you thought you could pass through.

All night you kept watch, in the United States of *How Are You Feeling?*, where fluorescent bulbs sizzled, struck threads of lightning above you. Self-starved, indignant, you overturned trays while nurses dressed like astronauts shuffled around your bed. Each time you screamed, white coats rushed to watch the "Lost Boy" trauma. Though they tried to look solemn, I swear they could hardly hide their glee, such exotic displays of PTSD!

When they finally left, we sat in the dark, the blizzard slamming itself against the window. Though we weren't supposed to (on account of your fragile psyche), we opened each other's childhoods anyway. And though our histories were not supposed to congeal (on account of my privilege, on account of our differing color of skin), let alone take to each other, our pasts grafted together into some clumsy mutation, some cross-cultural Quasimodo that limped around the room, made us laugh.

Later, despite the conspiracies I knew still whipped around your lonely skull, when the meds hit, your eyes rolled back, and you fell into what should never be called sleep,

I told you of the goodness even the snowy owls hold in their claws as they swoop the winter sky blood hungry. I cradled your shaved skull with the tenderness meant for a robin's egg. I even sang, in fact, I was so good at it, all night even the owls looked longingly through our window.

While Teaching Anthropology Class, I Think of Indra's Net, My Mother, and Try to Redefine ADHD

Suspended above the palace of Indra is an enormous net that extends
infinitely in all directions. A brilliant jewel is attached to each of the knots
of the net. Each jewel contains and reflects the image of all the other jewels
in the net, which sparkles in the magnificence of its totality.
—The Avatamsaka Sutra

On campus, the cold begins to doubt, contemplate pulling up stakes, the earth shifting its weight. In March, we are all a bit antsy, grumpy, giddy, mad with sun hunger, the bully of one season not quite giving in to the other. I walk around untethered, beneath the moody clouds, above the cracked sheets of ice with their contagion of trapped bubbles, water swelling everywhere, borders broken, green shoots raw with envy for more.

So much of us is not solid, or linear, a stormy alchemy, it's a miracle we fool ourselves into solidity each day.

Another student diagnosed with ADHD. My entire class on Ritalin. I want to rescue them from the land of the disordered, remind them at any given moment, we are multitudes, we are the jewels of Indra's Net, reflecting and refracting stories, wars, media, seasons, commercials, Twitter, sunlight and shadow, prayers and lies. They are simply manifestations of evolution's new self, it cannot be otherwise. Long gone the campfire, perhaps this is the new spark of evolution. We have evolved to carry contradictions that strike against each other, multiple truths sputter, combust and fire.

Gone, gone, gone beyond gone are the days of single selves, thoughts, and moods. Perhaps this is no disorder, but the great fireworks we were meant to achieve.

Through the class window I watch three wild turkeys poke their way through the campus lawns, pecking at the milky white grubs. My mind darts with ten thousand minnows. I want to tell them this is perhaps my mother's last spring. As I teach I am holding the weight of anticipated grief in a teacup so I don't shock anyone, just as I am lecturing on death rituals, while trying to focus on the present, an outdated term. The present. The present no longer comes in bulk form, but is spackled now, fractured, fickle, and I skip from jewel to jewel feverishly sucking nectar where I can. I show them *National Geographic* films that will mingle and refract with all the other realities in the vast nets of their being.

Suddenly I remember I forgot to give them a trigger warning as I'm supposed to do, when showing the tail ends of the life cycle, the deaths we inject with great vats of formaldehyde. Trigger makes me think of Tigger, who boings about with Pooh. If only students had such sturdy coils.

I describe a Tibetan Sky Burial: བྱ་གཏོར་ / *bya gtor*, literally "bird-scattered," a funeral rite where a chopped human corpse is placed on a mountaintop to decompose, exposed to the elements, eaten by carrion birds. I do not tell them that just as I fear death, I crave the decided peck of their beaks breaking up my flesh, that the visceral contradictions to live and to die lie in the same smelly nest. These days Chinese tourists flock to watch the giant vultures peck at the hacked human bodies. It is the second stop on a dark tour from which their Instagram will swell like a tick and prosper. They press in, feverish, with iPhones, trying to snap the most gruesome shot, so aggressive the monks can no longer carry on their sacred burials. You see? One ritual, simultaneously sacred and profane. Everything multiple things at once. In class their phones blink and vibrate in their pockets, the light leaks through their eyes. I cannot hold them in place.

I describe the Toraja, where the dead are kept at home for months and treated as part of the family, given lavish meals, water, even cigarettes to smoke. The children sleep next to the corpse at night, the parents talking and praying to them, the sick spirit of the dead craving attention, lingering until the death ceremony is held. I do not tell them of the multitudes that wrestle in my body, how fiercely, but furtively, I am practicing, rehearsing for my own mother's death as I play the faithful daughter. How at night I sneak up the stairs, crawl in beside her warm curled body as she sleeps, following the clotted flow of the breath that still gurgles faithfully in and out of her, caught by the wet uvula that hangs like a Venus flytrap from the ceiling of her mouth. I join my breath with hers and we cycle the night together, two sweeping owls, an act of solidarity, of simple union. I do not tell them of my predicted madness, the savage rattling of my body's rickety cage when her breath finally stops. How I will try and let the grief pass through me, how it will be fought, how it will torment and annihilate, soothe and disperse nonetheless. How it will be laced with culture, capitalism, and the truths Google sends me based on its read of who I am.

No longer can my mother accompany me and the dogs on our soggy stomping through the spring woods. I send her pictures from my iPhone—honey clusters, chaga, oyster, chanterelle mushrooms, sprouting from the rotting gray birch at our pond, whose pink bark is raw and wet and falls through my fingers like striated meat. I am both in the woods and not in the woods, simultaneously. Beware the *Amanita mascaria*, my mother always told me, knowing I had a penchant for placing juicy bits of the woods in my mouth. She never minded how close I wanted to be to the world, even when I tried to eat it.

It has been happening more and more. Supposedly separate orbits mingle and collide in my mind. Time and space morph within my body. In midsentence, midlecture, I envision my mother's ninety-year-old body draped across the forest floor. I am writing the assignment on the board, but obsessing on how she should be laid out, what I will sprinkle over her, how I will gently caress her puffed cheeks, what she will sprout up as, after she is taken by the soil's mycelial webs. Trillium? Trout lily? Back to the board. Should I lay her in a cold or warm glove of soil, on top of moss, mud, or beach leaves? Should she be placed in the hollow of a tree? Will the bones of her body be stiff as a rocking chair or slip loosely in the socket? Will her skull break like an egg, the yolk draining gloriously into the moss, the fox greedily licking her up? Will the flaxen milkweed of her hair disperse with the birds in clumps or strands? Will it be blown off easily like the white pappi of dandelion? Whatever it is, it will be beautiful, and I will see it as beautiful as much as I am destroyed by it, because everything is everything at once.

Back to class. The sun pours in a window while the oily ripping of a military jet tears above so loud I can't be heard. I pause. All of us gently simmer. Russia invades another bit of Ukraine. A new strand of COVID squirms into an unassuming cell. Serotonin slips past a synapse.

In Mongolia, the words *god* and *sky* are held by the same word, *Tengri*. At death, wind spirits usher the soul back to the timeless and infinite sky god. I do not tell them about my own sky, my mother, the pale green-eyed sky above me, the now-cloudy ceiling under which my entire world still revolves. I simultaneously think and question whether every mother is nothing less than the sky the child plays under, giving them a shelter from the infinite. My *Tengri*, the face of my mother, I do not know how to make her anything less epic, less final, less solid. Do you? Time to wrap the lecture up. Though they sit politely, already the students' bodies are humming with leaving. After they go, I stand at the podium, wallowing in the vibrations left behind. I contemplate what I crave for lunch, and underneath, the teacup quietly shatters—what will I do, will any of us do, when that sky leaves, the universe itself cracks open, and there is nothing left to keep us from slipping from this world?

Ethnography of Horror, Domesticated

NEW YORK CITY AND UNDERHILL, VERMONT

It was August in New York City, it had just rained, smell of garbage and sour milk. Late one night through our window, the dull thuds of punching. Rising up, a gurgle, like a small brook, of body fluid driven up the throat. The moans, mouse high and light as milkweed. Two doors slammed, the car screeched off. An eeriness that hung about, but not for long. After excusing itself briefly, the night gathered its skirts and sat up straight again, whisking any crumbs off its lap.

The next morning, the blood pennies sprinkled about the sidewalk shone a bright red, cheery as a child's finger painting. The rest of the blood had been sprayed away.

Back then it took very little for my mind to revisit my father's gruesome death. Without having been there, without getting to visit him while he was in a coma, my mind could only throw metaphor after metaphor on the incident, hoping one would stick. I never saw the news the night they showed his crash. I only have my imagination—lean god with stunning profile splayed across the metal gills of the car, scrunched like an accordion, my blood-spattered mother trying to pry him out in pieces. My father groaning through bubbles and foam, moans surfacing light as fairies. His limp spine draped like a Dalí clock on the steering wheel, broken jaw flapping like a porch door in the wind.

The day of the accident, I was in fourth grade when Mrs. Farmer pulled me from the Underhill Central school lunchroom of sloppy joe steam. I was aggressively licking the sides of my Devil Dog's vanilla crème, hoping to run out early to recess. Mrs. Farmer whispered that we needed to go home, her puffed cheek against mine. She smelled like weakness, like adrenaline had been nibbling at her insides. I knew her body had been feasted on by shock. She exhaled completely, the horror busting through the mouthwash, rotten like the mushrooms that covered our woods. She told me nothing, but I knew there was something tragic housed inside her, coming for me.

When I shimmied into the front of her Chevy, I felt my body stay, while my mind flew to some distant planet, until only a small black speck of it remained on the seat beside her. My mind alert, calculating, black hole dense, waiting for the predator to reveal itself further. I later called it *spider mind*, crouched and suspicious, ready to flee to the farthest edge of its orbit at the smallest touch of its web, ready to look down on planet earth with laser suspicion and a strangeness that startled me.

After they told me, the horror spread down Kusserow Road, all across Beartown Road, down into the stained-glass gloom of the Catholic church, then moved on to Pleasant Valley and River Road. It went where it felt at home first. To my best friend's house with her own dead father and gaunt, chattering birdlike mother. I could feel the horror sink into the sad autumn light, the slumped shoulders of hills, the quiet, unassuming moss.

From then on, it ran out of places to spread, so it moved into houses, schools, and stores unmarked by tragedy. It got so desperate it went inside the slick cafeteria at Browns River Middle School, where the students shrugged it off and kept eating their bologna sandwiches. It even tried to assault the guidance counselor. But she would have none of it. She knew where to put horror, to slap it with a DSM label, while slipping me a pill with a *V* on its back, and letting me hide in a closet that smelled of ammonia.

After that I had a disorder that barked like a sergeant. Directions, protocols were to be followed, experts consulted, therapist guidelines to be followed, pills swallowed. Each time my horror's raw scream tried to jump out, it saw no one it knew, turned around, and jumped right back into that DSM label, feeling stamped, cramped, and lonely, but accepting it as my fate.

During the long dark months of his coma days, the town felt like a factory, one that I wasn't allowed to work in, only to receive packages from, each house boxing up the horror of my father's death in Tupperware and Amazoning it out in sympathy that stunk of plastic wrapping. So that summer I hung out solely with my friend who'd been gutted by her own father's overdose when she was still grade-school pudgy.

We took to the woods, we let the earth absorb what school, hospital, and church couldn't deal with. We took the slipcovers from her mother Mary's chairs, placed them on our heads like nuns' habits, and walked the vast stretch of field up to Casey's Hill.

Even then we must have sensed who might be able to handle our horror. Nuns and nature. We figured nuns knew what to do with tragic unexpected death, so we mimicked them as we walked. The solemn vespers, the candles. But we were pagan nuns, opting for the moon, birchbark, moss, fairies, newts, and stone. At the top of Casey's Hill we'd rotate and face the moon, and chant something solemn. We were drawn to whatever stayed undone, opened, leaking, raw, yeasty, to whatever could not close itself. Grief rose from us, like the smell of baking bread. While everyone else was too busy to follow us into the woods, only the dogs followed tight at our heels.

In the end, I remember the black figures spotted about the hill where we put my father into the earth. Like feeding a baby, spooning the coffin deep into the soil. Shadows big as whales slid across the fields. The earth opened, the body forked in, stiff and white in its box. My father would stay down forever, swallowed by the Northeast Kingdom, worked on, worked on in ways I wasn't supposed to imagine.

It was in the hasty cover-up of the casket that I felt my violence surge, a repugnance toward the oncoming flock of docile but well-meaning sympathies, the laying on of manicured hands, of gentle, meek hugs that repulsed me, their soothing and coddling I wanted to kill, swat back like flies, and run.

So I ran away.

Listen, if you want to keep your children around, next time, lock this town down before it reaches to soothe and tame. Let the horror be fully consumed, digested, but still misunderstood—let it bust open the sutures of our understanding, then very, very slowly move on.

One Life to Live

RESIGNATION SYNDROME: A dissociative syndrome that brings on a catatonic state that can last for years, initially found among Balkan, Yezidi, and Soviet child refugees in Sweden after learning they have not been granted asylum.

Who knew that after hearing her asylum was denied, Ayen, too, would lie on her couch in a coma, catatonic, her toddler bouncing her Barbie down the length of her stiff, long legs. Who knew the psyche could be so clever! Playing 'possum until danger passes. Who knew trauma worked through bodies with such cunning, laying waste to beds of zombies, feeding tubes snaking through their bedsheets? Who knew, sometimes when war rolls over, like a grumpy lover, only the top of the psyche sticks to its back, the unconscious left mute and leaking behind?

All day we sit with her. Her vitals normal, nothing to do but wait, the head doctors say, talk to her of happy things, Abuk's new tooth, Deng's new job. Push her wheelchair to the dinner table, close to the steaming white rice, cup her hand, and help her draw a picture of the sun or a Dinka cow. Finally Ayen rises to the surface, mumbling. Whether she floated up upon hearing the theme song of her favorite soap, *One Life to Live*, or clawed her way onto the rescue limb of the nurse's chipper blood pressure read, she does not remember.

Whether consciousness can be baited and lured back up once it's sunk like an anchor, *We don't really know. Hard to say just what entices,* the white coats say. *What we do know: the courage to swim up, coaxing her to the surface, is often found mostly in a mother's voice, tones of hope transferred to the child.*

Now that she is upright, awake, her dizziness gone, the social workers deem Ayen "grounded," good to go, for now, the war settled like sediment to the bottom of her cells. But once inside the body, does war move up or down? Does it, too, succumb to gravitational pull? Maybe the body pisses it out, maybe it dissipates, like sweat and fog.

At home, when hunger for her mother's fish *kajaik* makes her salivate, from the Comcast menu Ayen eats and eats, lifts the remote worn smooth as a stone from rivers of hands, bathes in the giant technicolor TV, spread like a blooming aquarium across their wall, displacing somber frames of Dinka generals who just betrayed her anyway.

The social workers say too much TV is bad, a kind of repression of what needs to come out. Talk therapy is best. Healing is vertical, the bad stuff must rise up and out. But I don't tell her to stop. Together we sink into their giant Salvation Army couch, Abuk's chubby limbs slack across ours, Ayen resting deep in the underworld of *One Life to Live*, its vast, quiet mansions, clinking ice, swish of gowns. She falls asleep, the shrieks of war compressed into gentle, distant moans, like whale songs on the *Nature* show, sliding through the deepest parts of her mind, and slipping out somewhere, maybe even deeper, but finally beyond.

Stale Refugee

WINOOSKI, VERMONT (WITH "LOST BOYS"
OF SOUTH SUDAN)

THE LOST BOYS OF SUDAN were over twenty thousand boys of the Nuer and
Dinka ethnic groups displaced or orphaned during the Second Sudanese Civil
War, many of whom were resettled in America in 2003.

I see him cross the street, hobbling with a cane. Face puffy with opioids. I
haven't seen him since the accident, after he dropped out of high school, got
hit by a car as he was drunkenly weaving across the street. On disability now.

I pull my car over to say hello in Dinka. *Yikadee!* He pulls his earbuds out,
jokes, *No one wants me now . . . . remember when everyone wanted to talk to
me?* They still do, I say, and, feeling ashamed, vow to drum up some students
to pay him a visit.

It's true. At first they dropped by all the time, the church ladies, the
anthropologists, the students, the local reporter. They all left elated, having
found something real, like yoga and organic food. But different refugees go in
and out of vogue in this town, the newspaper wants fresh, not stale trauma.

The first Thanksgiving, three families booked him. Leaning hungrily across
the long white table, they nibbled at his stories, his lean, noble life. Over and
over he told them about lions, crocodiles, eating mud and urine, their veins
pumping neon fascination, deep in the suburbs, his life flavoring theirs, spicing
up supper, really, like a bouillon cube of horror. At the dinner table, the more

of what they now called *trauma* he remembered, the more the Americans came alive, with a sad, compassionate glow, a kind of sunset inside them.

He remembers the airplanes belching bags of food from their guts, the dust mushrooming up around a sack of cornmeal as it thudded and slumped over, like a fat woman crying in the sand. As he speaks, he is monitoring what would be of most interest, what will perk up even the boy from his phone. He decides to edit out a boring memory.

When he got off the plane the church ladies took him to a store, bought him fresh sneakers soft and white as wedding cake. The next day he walked through whole aisles of pet food, pictures of cats lounging like kings and queens on their couches.

Now he looks like a too-tall gangster, all gold chained and baggy trousered. The church ladies give him hushed looks: *We regret to inform you, the path you've taken is not what we had hoped for.* He's channel surfing, listening to Bob Marley, his long legs awkwardly pushed out to each side of the TV. Sudan's moved inside him now, all cramped and bored, sleeping a lot. He cracks another beer, starts to float, the reggae flooding his body. His cousin calls, she needs more money, her son has malaria. She can't afford school fees.

⊕

Later, he stumbles drunk into the bathroom. Inside him groggy Sudan flinches at the neon light, paces, then settles in the corner of its den, paws pushing into the walls of his ribs with a dull pain.

The next morning he wakes, stubborn Sudan still shoved up against his ribs, refusing to roll over, into the middle of himself where he can't feel it anymore, into some open place where he ends and a new America finally begins. He wants the old America back, where the freshness of his trauma was sniffed out like raw meat. Rolled in. Chewed in big chunks. He wants to be wanted again, for anything.

What Counts as Trauma

COLCHESTER, VERMONT

Of course it smelled inside the nursing home, moist and zoo-cage stale, two old men clustered near the nurses' station, wheezing.

Two others lay diapered, on cots, all claw and bone, stiff tendon and vein, taut neck strings exposed and vulnerable as the dried roots of overturned trees. Both stunned, as if expecting another fierce wind.

It was unbearable carrying Ana and Willem down the hallway, still hoo-hooing, their blonde ringlets bouncing, exotic eyelashes batting at those white stalks of death. I kept wondering if bits of our sweet life from the car stuck to our clothes, like fruit flies cling to a juicy peach, we were that ripe, that fresh, that joyous. We were singing "I See the Moon, the Moon Sees Me" as we barreled down the highway toward you. And though we did our best to dampen the glee so as to match the grim interior, we still were moist enough for their gazes to stick.

We walked into your room, Jane, my sweet Jane, my love, slumped in your wheelchair looking drunk, cheek still bruised, your lungs eerily singing as your wig slid like mud into one eye. You were panting fast as a dog, I didn't know if you would make it, if I could watch this, you started to babble and bat your hands motioning for Ana to come into your arms. I was afraid she would scream, shaming your last conscious hours.

So I locked my gaze into hers, my eyes saying, *Please don't cry, please don't cry*, then lowering her down gently into your bed of urine and saliva, the feeding tube gurgling with plasma, sprouting thick as weeds.

Frightened, she held onto my gaze like a child descending by rope into a well she does not know has a bottom. You smothering her with your hungry hands, clumsily rocking her like an ape with a toy, she struggling to get out. For all we knew, you had hours to live and now Ana was shrieking, like you were a circus freak.

Five years later, back in Vermont, it was learn about your parents' career day with the other kids at my daughter's school. This being a homeschool cooperative, of privileged kids, raised on flower metaphors (blossom, grow, sprout, bloom, unfurl), we had the luxury of taking field trips. *My mother is an anthropologist*, said Ana, proudly. I told them I went to faraway places and tried to understand them from the inside out. But anthropologists don't always go far away, they can go to places nearby. Take the elderly or local refugees. That's where I sometimes go. I was excited to take them to the Green Mountain Nursing Home with bunches of vased tulips my husband had grown.

Nothing prepared me for the terror and fear the children displayed, the way they clung to my thighs, afraid of the elderly. Some of them, in their fledgling psychospeak voicing their personal discomfort, were angry. Nothing prepared me for the way the elderly silently drank in their horror, accepting such reactions as their fate. Or the trauma I was later accused of causing. The parents came after me, *How could you? You should have known better*.

I do not blame the children. I do not blame the parents. I blame the quarantining of the tail end of human life. How in this organic-garden, back-to-the-farm, buy-local town, even rotting compost with its mold and sour heat held a noble seat in the order of things, a purpose and a legitimacy the elderly would never have.

Trauma, Inc.

BURLINGTON, VERMONT (FIELDWORK)

PTSD Questionnaire: Given to South Sudanese refugee girls in Uganda as well as my Introduction to Anthropology class.

Questionnaire Responses: My students score significantly higher for PTSD than South Sudanese girls.

I'm in Burlington, Vermont, with students from my anthropology class, invited to help local refugees tell their story at a writing workshop.

We sit in a circle. Bosnia, Sudan, Bhutan, Congo, Afghanistan, Somalia. Some of them say, *I'm Congo, I'm Sudan,* to introduce themselves. The leader cuts them short, *Oh, but what is your* real *name?* She wants them to know they are worth more than a generic country, that they should take pride in their uniqueness. And so begins the gentle wood whittling of the self at the hands of the well-meaning.

The air is filled with awkward, teacup delicacy, hushed phrases, knowing glances that suggest the writing coaches all know these refugees are trauma- tized with a capital *T*. Hesitancy crouches everywhere. The refugees don't know it yet, but soon Trauma will blot out any other master status (mother, survivor, cook, wife, healer, educator) they take pride in. Trauma will bully *resilience* out in favor of delicate, damaged views of self that depict fragility.

1. Do you think that something dangerous or frightening that happened may soon happen again?

The workshop leader, a soft-spoken local poet, emphasizes how they don't have to say anything they don't want to, that this is THEIR story, if they feel overwhelmed and need to process they can just hold up their hand midsentence and we will all understand. *It's important you respect your limits and honor how you feel*, she says to them kindly.

2. Do you have trouble falling asleep or staying asleep?

Due to the hesitance of the psychosphere, whose cushioned ground rules are being laid out with mind-numbing slowness, the refugees grow bored. They have taken time from their night jobs to attend this. They are losing pay. They want to write a story that gets published, their name in large print! They want their families back home to be proud!

I lock eyes with a pregnant Dinka woman, Bol, whose name means "born after the birth of twins." She is one of the first "Lost Girls" to arrive in Vermont, fierce, funny, eye rolling, robust, and tall, wearing a shiny wine-colored dress that looks like a ball gown. Her taut and bulbous belly like a bright pomegranate. She just wants to get on with it.

3. Do you often feel angry or lose your temper?

She raises her hand. She wants to tell a story about the time she was beaten by her husband.

OK, do you think you are OK with this? Is it too much? asks the leader. I want to warn Bol, read her her Miranda rights: she has the right to remain silent, anything she says can and will be subsumed by the well-meaning Traumasphere.

We break into partners for greater privacy. I'm paired with her since I've worked in South Sudan. I watch the entire workshop through her eyes now.

Finally, it's sharing time, again, the hedging, the protective gear applied to the damaged, delicate self (*but only if you want to, it's up to you, ask yourself if it feels like too much*). Soon the self looks like a padded hockey player on Halloween. The refugees shift and squirm with the presentation of ten thousand personalized and psychologically sensitive options.

4. Do you often feel like you can't sit still?

She tells me she wants to end her story with how she deserved to be beaten. She insists this was no *unjust* beating. She was being cruel to her children, horrible and unkind to her husband. Her cousin beside her nods, it's true. When the case was taken to the Dinka elders, they decided the beating was legit. The women both agreed.

5. Before the age of eighteen, were you ever physically punished or beaten by a parent, caretaker, or teacher so that you were very frightened or you thought you would be injured?

I watch her story hang in the air, unable to fit anywhere in the American creative writing landscape.

After the refugees leave, the workshop leader wants to debrief. The coaches huddle. Pity for the refugees settles like a gentle snowfall.

6. Do you ever have lots of thoughts or memories that you don't want to have?

I walk home, feeling defeated, discouraged. The widening of the trauma-psychosphere, displacing indigenous stories, the lush and intricate local responses to war that have taken years to evolve, with one story that preaches a frail and tender self stuck in reverse.

Trauma, Inc. is ravenous and cocky, it knows it's got a good thing going. It snorts whole white lines of history, religion, politics, removing them from the context of suffering.

7. Do you ever have bad dreams about something dangerous or frightening that happened to you or that you saw happening to someone else?

These days, more than food, we send in mental health experts to stalk the refugee camps. They move through, teaching survivors how to separate thoughts from emotions (which their culture has sloppily *lumped* together). It's called *mental health literacy*, where the Global South is saved by white professionals with DSM bibles. They are patient, in an eerie Flannery O'Connor way, spreading the word of the damaged self.

I think of the urgent email I received the day before from an American social worker in Kampala. The Sudanese refugee girls we sponsor are failing at the boarding school where we transferred them after civil war hit Yei. *What if it's trauma, how will we pay for a therapist?* Unlike the Kampala girls, Sudanese girls spend winter/summer break in refugee camps back in South Sudan, not a lot of English there. But it feels sacrilegious to suggest their failing is perhaps a matter of English proficiency.

8. Do you have a hard time paying attention?

Years later I run into Bol, now a licensed nursing assistant at Kindred Healthcare with four children. She is still perceptive, radiant, and cunning. She watches my pouting son obnoxiously tugging at my dress. He is whining, interrupting. I ask him to say hello, and he says he doesn't *feel* like it.

9. When you think about something frightening that happened to you,
   do you have bodily reactions such as a racing heart, upset stomach,
   sweating, or dizziness?

It's not just the refugees, but all across America, all across this campus, this liberal Vermont city, that the trauma bible spreads, to Head Start programs, required job trainings, day care centers, church basements, maternity wards, through our preschools and deep into the throats of university deans. The hegemony of the delicate, the wounded self, with its seductive flower metaphors, has taken root, in my own children no less, as I am a carrier, too, even though I try my best not to be.

10. When things happen all of a sudden that you weren't expecting, does
    it make you jump or become upset?

When the workshop is over, my well-meaning students and I, all of us white, pile into the college van, strangely quiet. And then, a kind of confession begins. *What if, what if . . . what if I offended my writing partner*, they ask, the fragile self hovering, swallowing them in its cloak of doubt. They speak in that hesitant way, a question mark tail curled up at the end, as if they are tiptoeing on trigger-filled terrain. What else can they do? I tell them Bol told me in the grocery store that some of the local Somali high school kids are using trauma to circumvent their parents' authority, get out of discipline. *They are wild*, she says, *uncontrollable, the parents are afraid to punish them, thinking they might go to jail*. My students don't buy it, don't recognize this pragmatic version of refugee.

11. Do you often worry about the possibility of dangerous or frightening
    things happening to you or someone you know?

And though my students do not speak, I can hear them.
Yes, they say,
Yes, we do.

The Day I Really Became
an Anthropologist

UNDERHILL CENTER, VERMONT

I was nine years old. My father still a handsome, lanky Prussian god when the 18-wheeler crushed his green VW bug. After that I changed planets and all was new and strange. Most days I was dealing with the terrors of my body, the sudden sweating, the crawl of coy, prickled dread up my spine, blossoming through my chest, the rocket blast of diarrhea, blouse drenched in sweat, rush to hide the shame.

I knew I was a freak, but I had to survive on this planet, so I watched my classmates doing their human things, nonchalantly, eating their lunches, passing notes in class.

I didn't like climbing around the cold, sticky edges of my cave all fucked up and lonely like Gollum. So when I had to be conscious, emerging like a corpse from my Valium/Benadryl haze, I tried my own version of participant observation, kickball at recess, hot lunches, Girl Scouts, bumpy bus rides, and tag. I tried focus groups, four girls giggling at an overnight I hosted once a week. I studied them. I did whatever they did, my sole mission to analyze their speech, tone, body language, smell, rhythm, my own cells absorbing their logic. I'd bait them with questions and watch the spool of their rationales unwind, the ones they took as normal, natural.

That's when I really became an anthropologist. When I could answer any question in the way they might, by ad-libbing off their chill philosophy of life, the base layers even they weren't aware of.

I called it *burrowing*, sneaking inside the mind's caves, viewing the landscape from their perspective. Strangely, it made me feel physically warm. I grew addicted to that feeling, to the point where I'd space out in class.

Participant observation. You plunk yourself in the middle of the bush in South Sudan, a high school in Bhutan, an NGO in Darjeeling, working and playing beside them but simultaneously observing. When you catch yourself getting a little lopsided (too much getting lost in their world, or too much standing aside and observing), you have to lean the other way. It's a delicate balance I've spent my whole life perfecting, I'm not sure how I could ever turn it off.

Skull Tree Stories

LOST BOY REFUGEE COMPOUND,
KAMPALA, UGANDA

One by one, skinny and solemn, in Salvation Army suits, scarred foreheads, the Lost Boys told their stories in long, formal Dinka orations. Arok, Malith, Ayen, Atem, Bol, Chol, Jurkuch, Deng.

Here, public stories are owned and run by men, the women kept quiet, to the sides.

Here, a story is the violence of the past flowing through you, the personal dissolving.

Here, a story links you to the strong and wide current of history, the ebb and flow of endless war.

I could tell I was far from home, far from the personal, therapeutic story, or the dramatization of the Freudian unique.

The story:

Hiding from the Arabs in the branches of a tree, two weeks surviving on leaves, legs numb, mouth dry. When the mosquitoes swarmed and the men's bodies settled limp as petals under the trees, they shinnied down, scooping out a mud pit with their hands, sliding into it like a snake, their whole body covered except their mouth. Perhaps others were near them, lying in gloves of mud, sucking bits of air through the swamp holes, mosquitoes biting their lips, but they dared not look.

One by one, through story, they linked themselves to South Sudan's black rivers of boys, their edges swelling and thinning as they wound their way over the tight-lipped soil, sun stuck to their backs. To villages pockmarked with bombs, Skull Trees with their necklaces of bones, packs of Lost Boys roving like hyenas toward Kenya, tongues, big as toads, swelling in their mouths, the sky pouring its relentless bombs of fire.

The story did not want to differentiate or congratulate, splice apart the living and the dead, the conscious from the unconscious, cull the brave from the weak. The story refused to mark them as different from the dead. The story never hung around any one place for too long, fixating, analyzing. Too much terrain to cover, politics to absorb. The story resisted the individual as hero or the celebration of those few who made it. Here, sticky personalities did not wind their righteous coils around the plot.

Each of them emphasized that, like the others, of course they were tempted to lie down for a moment, under the lone tree, with its barely there shade, to rest just a little while before moving on, the days passing slyly, hallucinations floating like kites above them, while the blanched bones of others no different from themselves lay scattered in a ring around the tree, tiny ribs, skulls, hip bones—a tea set overturned, as the hot winds whistled through them as they would anything, really, and the sky, finally exhausted, moving on.

Speaking in Tongues

Kickboxers

JUBA YOUTH CENTER, SOUTH SUDAN   *For Puro Okelo Obob*

One hundred fifteen degrees Fahrenheit. Four days before the 2013 coup. A dusty compound with a yard we could jog around, guarded by three Sudanese soldiers with AK-47s. I couldn't get myself to do it, strap on my Lycra, nothing more ludicrous than a white woman jogging off calories in a starving country.

Instead, I gawked at the kickboxers, enrolled in this *Tribe-less* program "aimed at lifting young men from the lure of street life and war." They pranced, sprang, kicked, and spat—a jet-black circus gang that looked hyped up on coke.

Their "gym," a huge mango tree with broken pieces of old donated barbells, elephant bars, rusty bumper plates, and free weights and one resident crippled dog. They trained with a fierceness, as if in trance, possessed—moaning, panting, squealing, a guttural speaking in tongues, biceps and calves nearly buckling in quick lifts, snatches, and squat jerks. Working whole continents of violence out of them one grunt at a time.

The sweat, the sweat everywhere, flicking off their bodies. I worried they would faint. One Dinka boy with no legs perched on top of his wheelchair, writhed agonizingly in and out of lifting a weight. I watched his torso buckle.

Underneath the heaviest elephant bell, his husky groans barely surfaced through his clenched mouth, sweat teetering over his bulging neck veins. Coach Puro fires off commands in Arabic: "Our TRIBE is Sport, no other Tribes allowed."

As new men came, they disappeared into a beat-up Porta Potty heaped with old American uniforms and pads, emerging fierce, strutting out like Mohammed Ali/Dinka Warriors in red, white, and blue boxing shorts. I knew they wanted me to look at them, so I looked hard, I never looked away, never for one second while they posed for me. I gave them the only appropriate gift, admiration. I staged mock wonder. I played Western Woman blown over with amazement, the guttural vowels of awe erupting when they held a stance, and held it trembling, Atlas style. What could they do with my pity, my critiques?

Bless this man, Puro, who had done it, found a competitor for the soldier, the drug, the glue, and the gun. This gaudy kicking parade of male swag, their boxed-tight determination, muscle-bulging sex and sweat musky thick with rebellion and ego.

During breaks they glistened and laughed, guzzling whole gallons of water. Coach Puro still training despite the war like a thundercloud in the distance.

Little did he know it was too late, as he leaned over, speaking into my recorder, angrily, as if it were housing a God who was hard of hearing or had deceived him too many times, *This boxing is the only way out of war, can't you see?*

The Fat Claw of My Heart

SUDANESE REFUGEE CAMP,
NORTHWESTERN UGANDA

Part African bush, part Wild West, we're based in Arua, grungy, dusty frontier town, giant diesel trucks barrel through, spreading their wake of adrenaline, obese sacks of grain lying like walrus inside. I chase Willem from malarial puddle to puddle, my white blouse frilled like a gaudy gladiola, my lavish concern for my chubby son suddenly rococo, absurd.

Our drivers gun insanely over the dusty red roads, lurching from pothole to pothole. A caravan of slick, adrenalized vans, tattooed with symbols of Western aid. Willem on my lap, trying to nurse between bumps, my hands a helmet to his bobbing skull. A three-legged goat hobbles to the side, and though we imagine we are a huge interruption, women balancing jerrycans on their heads face our wake of dust and rage as they would any other gust of wind—*Water, Sun, NGO—*

We arrive covered in orange dust, coughing, a fleet of SUVs parked under the trees, engines cooling, Star Trekkian cockpits flashing, alarms beeping and squawking as we zip-lock them up and leave them black-windowed, self-contained as UFOS. Behind the gate, we stumble through the boiling, shoulder-deep sun, Willem and I trying to play soccer as a trickle of Sudanese kids cross the road, hanging against the fence, watching the chubby *muzungu* boy I've toted around Uganda like a pot of gold. Three years old, he knows they're watching, so he does a little dance, his *Spider Man* shoes lighting up as they hit the dust.

Seven-foot giants of the Sudan People's Liberation Army huddle together, drinking, talking Dinka politics, repatriation, the New Sudan. Wives lanky as giraffes set food on the table and move slowly away. In candlelight, the men's forehead scars gleam, I flutter, acting more deferential than I'm used to, known as *Robert's wife*, I stick with the other wives in the back kitchen.

Slowly I'm learning Sudanese grammar: men are the verbs; women, the conjunctions that link them together. In the thick of rain we walk home, Ugandans huddled under their makeshift bird cages, Willem now pointing to the basic vocabulary of this road: dead snake, prickly bush, squealing pig, peeing child. Three drunk men sit under a shack, scrape the whiteness off us as we walk by. Though I don't want to hear it, though I love Uganda, it starts up anyway—rising up from guilt, the milky mother cells of my body high-fiving, my mind quietly repeating the story of my son's lucky birth, his rich American inheritance.

My husband drops into bed, dragging a thick cloak of requests. All day I've labored behind him, toting our clueless boy, watching him, Dogged Dutchman in his rubber clogs climbing the soggy hills of Kampala, despite the noonday heat, a posse of hopeful Lost Boys following him, he afraid of nothing, really, not even death, me afraid of everything really, most of all his death.

In the distance, trucks rev up to cross the bush, where Sudanese families, perched like kites caught in trees, wait for the next shipment. But it's night now, the three of us inside our guesthouse, the two of them next to me, breathing, safe. Willem's nursing again, though he doesn't need to, swelling like a tick, and though I don't want to feel it, the fat claw of my heart rises up, fertile, lucky, random, pulsing and hissing its victory song.

NGO Elegy

NUBA REFUGEE CENTER, YEI,
SOUTH SUDAN

Tucked inside the mosquito net's gauzy bubble, taut white fabric like a bridal dome, I can hear Amin, my translator, all drunken fire and brimstone from the throne of his broken plastic chair. At rehab, blond men with ponytails that look like women read him the gospel, hoping it will stick. But it never does. Now he's wild, busted sutures everywhere, gushing Red Army rage. Even Nuba soldiers avoid him as they drink hard at the bar. A six-foot Dinka prostitute dodges his drunken advance as she shuffles by in flip-flops, shooing him away like the flies scurrying in and out of the mouths of Blue Nile beers.

Thunder, rain, whole chunks of road gape open. USAID projects loosen, fall apart at the seams. Amid the pounce of rain, Taban, our night guard, bow and arrow at the ready, sleeps fitfully in the closet with the rats and frayed electrical cords.

Like the other expats, I doubt myself a hundred times a day, our efforts to help perhaps just more puppetry, in an endless play that has no plot, no meaning, no beginning, no eye *dhatu*, no ear *dhatu*, no *Post*, no *Modern*, no-*anthro*, no-*polo*, no-*gist*, only this country, with its sweet and terrible songs that hover like fog in giant capes of hope and doubt.

The next morning the fluorescent sun bleaches the crap out of the Congo road, cachectic men still sleep off hunger as the cicadas whine like sirens. In front of our dilapidated NGO, a Nuba boy looks up from his dopey malarial puddle as a land mine truck races by.

A tenderness passes between us that I am too tired to dissect or deconstruct, a brush of sweetness, the way a thrush beats quietly, across the night.

Those Days We Played God

YEI, SOUTH SUDAN AND UNDERHILL, VERMONT

One month after the Sudanese coup, we heard Machar's rebels had invaded Yei from an informant on the ground. Some of the Lost Boys and Girls' parents were trapped, all of Yei surrounded, the airport seized, all of the girls at our school blocked without food, no one could escape without rape or death. So we rallied our NGO board and brainstormed on conference calls from all over the United States. We decided the only option was to ship the girls out by armed convoy as one of the board members had access to huge trucks.

All of us were well schooled in the idiocy of white rescue, its lack of sustainability, etc., etc., but at this point it was all they had, these clueless *muzungus* pulling strings on the other side of the planet. Banned from the country, airports shut, we could only meddle from afar. It felt sickening, these Americans deciding their fate as we lay on our palatial beds at 2 a.m. And yet never were we so alive, coked up with mission. It put Christmas's cocky grin to shame. My husband and I walked back to the kitchen adrenalized, both of us trying to mask it from our kids, but it leaked through nonetheless, a kind of neon guilt. We were lit from within. And no amount of shame would keep us from glowing like jack-o'-lanterns.

You see, prior to this, materialism had deadened us, individualism had isolated us, made us puffy with self-concern, and if Viktor Frankl were to analyze us, he'd say we were definitely starved for meaning. It's no wonder we felt guilty, grabbing the magnetic pull of some other country's war. We'd stumble into the kitchen, stuffing in our stray adrenaline like shirttails, cinching our waists, tell our kids, in an attempted CNN monotone, the situation these refugee girls were in and what we were trying to do.

As they ate their cereal, a kind of suspicion settled on their faces, an anger almost, a frustration, somehow they knew they'd lost us then, glowing, playing God, high in the rafters, heroically pulling the strings of others' lives. For now, their parents had escaped the American Christmas capitalist hive and no longer found it pleasing. For now, they knew nothing in their middle-class school lives could compete.

Home of Confident Children
Out of Conflict (CCC)

JUBA, SOUTH SUDAN (AMERICAN WRITERS ABROAD,
US DEPARTMENT OF STATE EVENT)

The sun, the only dictator left standing now. Each day it begins its manic inquisition, full bore, relentless. You do not mess with the Sudanese sun. You can feel it drunk with power, bossing everything around, animals, humans, insects, rivers.

None of us knew, one week before the December coup, another civil war would torch and burn the capital. Adrenalized air, sharp, acrid tension that hovered and refused to land, absorbed by the tight-lipped streets.

We raced through Juba, they told us not to look anyone in the eye, even from inside our bulletproof van.

Outside the girls lined up for our arrival. They came from the cemetery, and Konyokonyo market, the slums. Most of them prostitutes, glue sniffers, no parents.

It's easy to spot them, the director said, they travel in groups, but you have to visit them over and over, for months, to gain their trust.

With us was the US ambassador and her dashing bodyguard, Domingo, and three burly, clean-shaven marines. We were there to read stories to the girls.

All of them, with shaved heads and donated T-shirts, gathered round, a kind of apathy on their faces that I imagined a story would do nothing to budge.

As the ambassador looked on, I read *A Snowy Day* and tried to describe winter in America. Still nothing budged, I had never seen faces so quiet and blank, an eerie stillness like the snow they knew nothing of.

I thought of the tyranny of bedtime ritual back home where parents emerged from the caves of their children bleary eyed and exhausted after the tenth bedtime story that the little ones demanded.

Meanwhile, the marines politely bought handmade earrings for their girl-friends and mothers back home. The ambassador danced in her indigenous purple dress.

Back in our hotel rooms, we collapsed in relief, sweat, and grief.

The day I left, the airport, an open-air market, littered, chaotic, filled with Chinese businessmen, pickpockets, and five-foot-tall trash-eating Marabou storks. Bald, beady-eyed storks, scalps scabbed with dried blood. Beneath their foot-long beaks hung huge pink air sacs, deflated balloons, feces dripped on their legs. Marabou, marching through the scum and garbage like skinny undertakers. So cocky, so meticulous, so almost human, like death draped on stilts, I worried they might eat a toddler.

I pushed to the front of the line, I held my bag so tight I could hardly breathe.

Finally, the plane lifted its nose into the blast of Sudanese sun. Goodbye, South Sudan, newest country on earth. Of course, the reading of stories never did cheer the girls up—after the fifth story did nothing to budge what perhaps should not be budged, I remember asking the girls what was their favorite food. Suddenly their faces exploded with glee,

RATS, they said. *RATS!*

·II·

We now have access, increasingly, to more and more cultures across the globe, and the result is that restlessness has gone global . . . the sense of an answer to be found somewhere else.

PICO IYER, *The Open Road: The Global Journey of the 14th Dalai Lama*

On the Brilliance of Your Story

BURMA, NEW JERSEY, AND VERMONT

PSYCHOPHOBIA: an aversion to psychological considerations.

Your fingers still bruise your rosary with mad devotion.

When you first came to America, your loneliness swelling high above the bus station, up where the angels lay, you built your makeshift apocalyptic nest, pulling in the cheapest Jersey gods that flew around, storm after storm, in that neon grim city.

Now, you are losing it, they say, paranoid delusions of soldiers breaking into your house. You hide your car from the police, clutching the hot vein of your cell phone as you drive your mother in her conical straw hat across the bumpy Vermont fields, staring out from her yolky Alzheimer's haze as the car lurches over the mud and leaves. I tell them to let you be, let you suckle on the story that heals, even if it's one they don't approve.

No one can weave as fiercely as you. You who never should have been exiled from Burma. You afraid to leave your apartment now, the isolation you say now suits you. You, in your tattered white bathrobe, gray roots frosting your scalp, peeking out from curtains, to see who might be there, like a spider sensing its web, pricked, wrapping each social worker in the pure white gauze and clouds of Jesus's paradise, as they look at you and speak to you of *maintaining healthy boundaries* with the tenderness reserved for an infant or a dog.

Once, you recalled for them the steamy jungles of your birth, the hell of your flight, where you ran and ran through the night and woke to a python wrapped around a tree, your father hacking its head off, prying its seventeen-foot-long body off the trunk. It took so long for it to die, to uncoil enough so you could feast on the eggs lined up like potatoes in its womb.

Though you tell them you are well, that reincarnation landed you with Jesus, they say you are in denial (a form of death, a blindness), talk to you of the dangers of *psychophobia*, show you a cartoon called "My Ego." What you really want to speak of is angels, the Holy Spirit, golden wings, dappled light, the latest issue of *The Watchtower*.

For now, who is to say what stories suffocate, or heal, which ones work or fall flat, which ones comfort us in the dark? The X-rays of your brain, with their gullies and black caves, may or may not save you. The stories they hurl to you for rescue can still let whole vats of plump suffering slide through their nets, as the white coats proudly drag you onto shore.

Oh, the brilliance of your story, they say, is covering up the real story. Don't let them belittle it, as you coax yourself home each night with the angels that calm you. Who is to say what holds you intact as you're hurled through space, landing with a thump into the great American refugee hive, and begin this frantic human work, perpetual manic revival, stretching your way through the half light of this vast unraveling strangeness?

I Watch My Daughter Snort Google

UNDERHILL, VERMONT

She's charged, alert, snorting quick coked-up bits of info, Snapchats pulsing like Vegas in her veins, strays of Twitter, texts, YouTube jamming her million neural pathways. Blinking neon billboards line the circuits of her brain, luring bits of stray ego into side alleys named *flashy*, *sexy*, *cheap*, *shocking*, *tragic*, *fun*!

I feel like a deer, all sniff and hesitance, hovering at the edges of her psyche's field. I resort to nagging, it's almost violent what it takes to lift her head from the screen. I touch her shoulder, she's quick to snap and flame, burning with impatience, frustration, greed, like flares along a highway telling me to stay away.

What happened to the dopey, unpopular emotions I grew up with, the ones that wobbled out onto the roads after a slick rain, the endangered ones, the slow and smelly ones, like empathy, like awe, sympathy, confusion, and grief, barely lifting their heads to sniff around before flattened like roadkill.

Yet, last night, it finally felt like spring, I watched her, pale and doughy, hungover on bytes, wade ghostlike into its free-floating green, despite her phone buzzing inside. The moon stuck to everything, pulling her with viscous milky threads. I watched her sink into the cold, wild blades of grass, mud and fiddle-heads, mineral, bone and bud. I swear I saw whole vowels of awe, rising from her mouth like bubbles, like Chinese lanterns, rising.

Bhutan

East Wants West Wants East

THIMPHU, BHUTAN   *For Lama Shenphen*

I'm back again, working for the government in the last country on planet earth
to get internet, here to preach the dangers of Facebook, Instagram, TikTok,
the sexy fictions global media spins about the West. The government calls it
selective modernization, letting in only the best of the West, but all I see are
guns, gangs, and actors bleached in *Fair and Lovely* on the tiny TVs now in
every store on this street They tried banning MTV, World Wrestling Federation,
Fashion TV, but now the flow is impossible to stop, the channels breeding and
multiplying. Even among the farmers far outside the city, satellite dishes cock
their chins south, magnets to the subtle, sly presence of Envy creeping into
houses like stray cats, coyly rubbing and curling around their hearts.

Each day I walk to the top of the Thimphu hills, where the sun leaves its
afterbirth everywhere, prayer flags drench the pines, a monk scampers away
like a red fox. Couples park their cars, condom wrappers are lodged doggedly
in the mud, asserting their rightful place in the path to enlightenment. Dingy
Indian buses, painted gaudy as prostitutes, careen around the battered road to
the capital, taking villagers to Thimphu, where, among youth, lust for the West
huddles like fog, packs of roaming boys dressed in black jeans and T-shirts

scour the streets for drugs, the ones who eye the Westerners hungrily, black eyes nibbling feverishly at the manic commercials flashing from the storefront TVs. These boys who failed their exams, left their farms, mocking their prune-faced grandparents huddled in dark corners mumbling mantras. They want computers not soil, Bollywood, not Buddhism.

Now they sit hungover at the dingy youth center, unemployed, faces pimpled and tired, confessing their shame to the Welsh monk who has made it his life to help them. Gutted and global now, the wet viscera of shame leaking from them. He sits patiently in his faded burgundy robes, trying to bring them back into the fold.

Meanwhile, tucked above the cobbled streets in the smoky Thimphu disco, at the OM Bar, CNN shouts its noble manifesto from its perch above the liquor, schools of ghostly European expats sway, waving their drunken limbs, lightheaded, wan from this geography of bliss. Geography of want. The Bhutanese boys snorting coke in the bathroom, emerging in black leather jackets and slicked-back hair, going straight for the Western girl who looks like Britney Spears.

After their treks, yoga, or meditation, the Westerners lay their drunken bodies down on the stiff hotel beds, where all night they try and meditate, let it go, let it go, and still they come back to this density of longing, hard kernel of desire where the bulky psyche chips its tooth and winces again, stumbling back to the breath.

Outside my window, deep in the alley below, the Bhutanese boy, high on meth, wailing a kind of love song for the West, while barking dogs mince the night 'til it bleeds.

Psychocolonialism

VICTORIA, HONG KONG

YAN SHI ZHENG: anorexia.

In Hong Kong, Jiao lies alone in her room, her bones laid neatly like kindling on her bed.

Too weak to rise, she floats in a haze of light-headedness, what Nai Nai* calls blocked qi, an excess of yin, a depleted yang. *How old-fashioned, how quaint.* She first stopped eating after Nai's hand went limp on the hospital sheets, cold as just-thawed chicken. That day, the hospital irises opened their furry throats, she wanted to crawl inside their yellow luminous caves, still as icefalls—she could not help but lick one, so she left quickly, a yellow petal poking from her mouth.

On the subway home after Nai Nai died, the jarring of the tracks lulled her. She picked a woman out, any one would do, exhausted after all these years. She wanted to be picked up like a mother dog grabs the slack of her loose-necked pup, to be folded up, and slid into the warm pink pocket of the woman's body, sipping at the walls of fat. She wanted to go back, eyes open in the warm fluid, lungs soft as petals, bones light as cartilage, before the shock of

* Grandmother.

sun blasts in and the waters recede, revealing the islands bright and stubborn, borders quickly staking their claim.

When she told the doctor of her longings, he told her the DSM had no diagnosis for symptoms like that. Now, she is a modern girl, with a modern illness, its capped teeth gawking from *People, Self, Vogue*. She knows it did not start this way, like the Western doctors described, but, tired of being lonely, her symptoms never *just right*, she learned the real ones eagerly, like a refugee scarfing down the language needed to survive.

The grammar of *yan shi zheng* took root, spreading its greedy tubers across her mind.

Now she's miserable, but fluent, swimming in the popular symptom pool so in vogue, a poster child for the disease. Like the parents of other girls, hers are worried, hovering like ghosts outside her door, respecting the *yinsi* (privacy) the American doctors say girls need.

At night, of its own accord, the snake of her mind slips out, slides over the day's caloric intake, obsessively, like a tongue runs over a cavity's new filling. Her fingers tracing the terrain of her skin, the prized rocky pelvis, her T-shirt absorbing the sweat of a psyche on lockdown.

Outside, the city nudges its grubby paws up through frost. Through the window, she smells hunger, gears shifting, a reluctant, rusty productivity, grinding back into life.

She obsesses on the irony of bodies—98 percent water, condemned to the life of a solid, the way spring makes her flesh a cage.

The Trauma Mantras

AMHERST COLLEGE, AMHERST, MASSACHUSETTS

Back from study abroad in Tibet, she's lonely. She no longer really fits in.

She was given a mantra by a sketchy monk, but she's already forgotten it. Fuck, what was it? She should use it, to soothe, focus, calm herself down from the Ritalin jitters. She tried *Om Mani Padme Om*, the McDonald's of all mantras, but it didn't stick. Without the chanting, the monastery, the circumambulation, it fell flat, her mind went back to wandering and worrying over its typical thorny landscapes.

Instead, she settles back with what she knows, her trauma mantra. She carries it with her everywhere, tucked in her pocket like a cell phone, from room to room, dragging it into bed, glued to its eerie light, ignoring her boyfriend as she recites the same old stubborn narrative, the same story of childhood damage. She fingers it like prayer beads. Worries when it will resurface. She feeds it meticulously like a mouse on a treadmill. Consults it under the desk so others don't see, uses it to explain the day's skip or limp.

In therapy, it keeps them both from getting bored, they return to it when there's a long pause, when language can't encapsulate her rogue mind or runamok moods or odd cravings for width and sky.

It keeps her oriented, her GPS in a dizzying world. She's terrified that without it she'll be left without a language, a psychological raison d'être.

Sometimes she panics when she senses it unravel, her axis mundi. She tries to give it up for a few days max, and oh the sadness/relief when reunited. She purrs, coos, licks it back into her lap. She loves the slow-drawn drama of licking her wounds. Simultaneously it frightens and grounds her. She lets herself be triggered by all manner of things, from the news to the classroom, her story blinking like a firefly across the vast dull soccer fields and frat houses.

She shares her trauma mantra, just enough to coax empathy, not enough to frighten others, get labeled a freak. It's a delicate balance, the cultivation and dissemination of one's suffering story. She scrolls through its plot, its cult of uniqueness, how it keeps her feeling special, heard, above all the generic, collective stress other students share. Amid the hierarchy of generic student stress-bragging, her mental pain reigns supreme.

In Tibet, her trauma story felt oddly small, tiny as an ant, at times irrelevant. It was the first time she tried on other stories about suffering. At first they swallowed her like baggy clothes, but gradually she felt them fit. Among the Tibetans, everyone shared a kind of acceptance of universal suffering. No one tried to vie for the prize of most pained, most medically exotic, no one won most destroyed or damaged, no one's suffering was off-limits or indecipherable to another human.

Back at school, when she wakes early in the morning, she hears her trauma mantra gather its wings, its song, like a lullaby, a loon off in the mist, a lost limb, a phantom, and a kind of longing fills her. *Come home, come home.* She gives in to its magnetic, seductive pull. She rolls in its distinct odor like a dog. She bites into its thick, musky meat. Without it, she fears a great unraveling into a vast cosmos, an untethering into something generic, diluted, and plain.

She scrunches under the blankets her mother bought her at Target, burrows back into the warmth of the trauma mantra, because, for better or worse, it's her home and she knows what to expect.

Here in America, it's different, your story needs to be special, but not enough to land you in the psych ward. Again, it's a delicate balance she's got to get better at.

Tulip Fever

I wander, light starved, into the thousand tulips my husband planted, just as they open their gaping red-and-purple jaws, just as the sun finally drags its paw across the mangy, battered meadows. What an indulgence, the farmers must say, as they bitterly whack the caked manure off their black rubber boots.

Still, how I love them with such desperate hunger. In their presence, my brain begins its frantic hunt, its ravenous pounce, an almost-violent pecking of metaphors, similes flocking in like a murder of crows. I used to think it was in the ritual of perfect description

I could be closest to them:

May 15: Burning Hearts, Queens of the Night, lipstick streaked, thighs splayed open.

May 16: Orange flames of the Fire Parrot, black beaked and wild, guzzling wells of ink down their necks.

May 17: Double-fringed white Angeliques, a whole squawk of geese flapping and nipping toward the sky.

May 18: Giant red Darwins, shiny-clawed lobsters, underbellies bulging
and blue veined.

And yet it was still a kind of torture to be separate from the tulips.

As a child, hoping to swallow their beauty whole, I sucked on a petal, a mammoth white lobe bringing nothing but a gagging fake communion.

I didn't know that something mute and elemental would open, as I sat throat deep in that field, and let the tulips be, a kind of quiet softening in the bed of my mind, that I would come to cherish for even five or six seconds, when all the crows stopped pecking and all the tender beauty of my husband's crop, by now pockmarked with such desperate description, finally stopped bleeding.

Field Notes

Nursing Home Fieldwork with Students

COLCHESTER, VERMONT

On the way to the nursing home, after Thanksgiving, talking about their lives of technological saturation, my students tell me they get so frustrated with their grandparents. *They're so slow*, they say.

Last time I brought them, an elderly man named Walter crumpled to the floor, the cut on his pink bald head juicing blood. Cracked lips milky with fear, his breath screaming a kind of poison adrenaline. We pried him from the wreckage while he thrashed about, as if surfacing from a bad dream.

Today, I see the students, glistening skyscrapers of a beaming youth culture, trying not to notice how weakened and bewildered he looks—as if the wind just blew off his hat, white tufts of hair stuck up like a duckling's tail, as he rights himself in his clunky boots, his paunched belly poking out between the buttons of his shirt. I notice they turn the other way when he looks like an elf—paddling around his room in the *hss hss* of his slippers, his blue eyes cloudy, pupils the size of pins, his depression the consistency of porridge.

They walk with him to the garden, his slowness a kind of agony they try and mask, tapping their fingers, clicking their pens, checking their phones, all efforts to try and nonchalantly drain the mania inside them. They know if they show any impatience, he'll wilt into silence. So they swallow back whole bodies of speed, frustration, restlessness, ones that rise despite their good intentions. I give them credit for the the ways they try and hide their agitation, distraction. They walk around with bulging cheeks, smiling, swallowing back the momentum they buzz with in the "real" world. I tell them it's what we do for our elders, we come back to them, after work, between classes, whipped up with speed and productivity, the swallowing, the swallowing day after day, the subtle hiding of the other worlds that whirl their sharp wings inside us.

Himalayan Facebook Fiction

DARJEELING, WEST BENGAL, INDIA,
AND JFK AIRPORT, NEW YORK

Tenzin eyes the three restless blond trekkers,
hairy limbs poked out from North Face pupas,
bad breath, sweat, impatience condense, bead the tent ceiling.
Fog huddles in, clouds block Everest, prayer flags sag.

He knows they prefer a kind of fucked-up fiction,
a *Himalayan Fantasy*, meanwhile, tea plantations wilt
with drought, dried sky sticks to bushes, traffickers comb
through the ruins, luring girls fed nothing
but Bollywood from the lone village TV,
like his cousin Pema, who woke up in a brothel,
pelvis sore as a gutted fish, now cleaning bathrooms
at Kennedy Airport as the trekkers
Namaste their way around her mop.

Glossing over the spring break vomit, she wrings her mind
of doubt and regret, earplugs blocking the violence
of flushes while the industrial toilets suck the shit away,

the smell of cleaner like poison to her eyes as she looks up,
as if through cataracts, to accept a tip.

At lunch break, she watches Fox News prance
its gaudy circus of stars, walks through the terminals,
where humans glisten with iPhones that deflect and protect,
brushing up against casual glances, nothing too human,
just the low magnetic pull of the bored cashier or the Starbucks barista.

Meanwhile, in Nepal, the fog thickens. To pass the time, the trekkers
burrow down to the roots of America's woes, comparing them
to a more noble Nepal Tenzin doesn't recognize. To tune them out,
he feigns meditation, working his prayer beads in the corner, Buddha style.

Behind his staged calm, a murder of thoughts erupt:
He could slash their fictions if he dared.
He's running out of fairy tales
to feed them, the ones they post like hornets,
stinging friends with envy. Still, he's no better,
wants Pema's bold and beautiful USA
to be real, swoons at her Facebook profile shot,
even though he suspects she, too, beams pretty lies across the web.
Fair and Lovely bleaching her face snow-white
as she floats like a moon high above the sparkling skyscrapers.

Prostrations

Black Lives Matter rally at the park, the speaker asks us all to get down on the concrete, facedown. So we do, the grit and dust of city cement in our mouth, *This is just a taste*, she says.

We make a show of our lack of hesitance—we are all so ready to punish ourselves in this liberal white town.

Suddenly I'm back in Boudhanath, where I had just drunk the water, hoping to get sick. I was restless, wandering from meaning station to station, like all the other bedraggled nomads fleeing the West. Back then, when I felt lost, I'd follow my body, let my mind drag behind like a well-meaning doll I'd outgrown. Each night, my body knew what I needed long before my mind. I went out to the stupa, hiding in the shadows of the closed storefronts, watching the Tibetans prostrate around it like inchworms, whole body stretched facedown on the ground.

Buddhist prostration starts standing upright, with the lotus bud mudra (the base of the palm and fingertips together) on the crown of the head, then moves to the throat and heart. Dropping the body forward and stretching it full length on the ground, the arms outstretched in front. Entire pilgrimages in a series of prostrations, standing, pressing their palms into prayer, stretching flat, scrambling to their feet, taking two steps forward, and repeating the whole process all day long. Wood slats on their palms protect skin as they slide.

Too embarrassed to do it in public, I practiced it in my room and my thoughts fell off so easily, like a husk revealing the joy of being small, being no one.

Sometimes you just need to place the body in archetypal positions, let the mind take its cue from the shape you inhabit in relation to the earth. It's not often we're taught to be small in this country, to humbly lower ourselves face down onto the ground. Or how beautiful it can feel, that is, if someone's boot isn't lodged in your neck, warm gun to the back of the head.

Love Poem to America, Quarantined

Inside their homes, to pass the time they burrow through Google, like moles, coiled on their beds, pale limbs wrapped around the screen, the way trees graft themselves to another species, no matter how foreign.

In fits of sleep, their fingers twitch at fake keyboards the way the eyes used to rove frantically over a dream.

And yet, despite the quarantines, their maddening monotony, they sing from balconies, laugh and joke inside their Zoom squares.

Deep inside the locked-down skulls, shocks of brilliance startle over and over, like a flock of birds that never rests. All night, their imaginations pulsing like fireflies.

I tell my children, no one loves humans more than I do, especially now, calling to each other like caged owls, their loneliness whittled into sound.

Poor humans, even though they've forgotten they're miracles, haven't they noticed, even their longing is so terribly beautiful?

What Makes Us (Not) Buddhists

LADAKH, NORTHERN INDIA, AND
UNDERHILL, VERMONT

In Ladakh, it's *tsha tsha* time, fields of monks and nuns chant, torsos bobbing, their mantras thick and shifting suddenly, in wild Buddhist murmurations. Monks in flip-flops shuffle from cremation pyres, hands filled with bone fragments from last winter's dead, smashing and grinding them with stone. Pulverized, mixed with silt and water, sprinkled with mustard seeds, packed into pudgy clay molds in the shape of a tiny stupa. They'll place the *tsha tsha* high in the mountains, to be pummeled by the wind and snow, crushed by the wild blue sheep as they pick their way through the cliffs and eroding soil. *Tsha tsha* are never meant to last.

It's late September in Vermont, the light like weak tea. We are all so sick of quarantine. My husband plants his tulip bulbs, their shape and color identical to the *tsha tsha*. He, stocky and stubborn, leaves the house in a huff, plants them fiercely, as a way to hang on, nailing beauty in place, a way to not let go. He digs and digs down nearly a foot, his shovel violent, his psyche swelling, on fire.

My mother, hungry for company, hobbles into the garden to watch him, tentatively, as if she is a burden, her spine bending in irrelevance, as if trying to duck under the entire world, her loneliness hanging off her like an old coat. He digs and digs with a kind of joyous violence. With each bulb he plants deep bombs, a nod to a stubborn, bullheaded beauty, a ritual *Fuck you* to all that threatens to oust it from this world. All winter he eyes them from his watch-tower, guarded by a high fence, cursing the rodents and deer, holding on until May, when their thousands of dark red tongues will rise and obliterate everything in their wake. Meanwhile, our prayer flags flutter, free-floating gills, sucking at the air, sharp, greedy.

Anthropology of American Yoga

The Dalai Lama Looks Down on a Yoga Class

NEW YORK, NY

Peering out onto the vast space, the universe with its sullen orange and pink mists, the planets hanging quietly as spiders, he finds earth, its bald, swirled head, its whirling cacophony, limping around the orbit like a disheveled bride, ozone clinging like an ill-fitted wig.

Earth, dragging its bumpy train of Chinese plastics, the refugees pushed up like rice to the sides of borders, the swarms, the migrations pulsing north, the bodies floating in flood after flood, the hissing and praying, humming and tingling, as miniscule embers of the internet glow.

In America, millions of dilated pupils absorb Kardashians, as Mexican children huddle in an ICE cage. Televisions squawk their bright lights, hawking shiny arguments.

In suburbs, pale teenage boys float like baby moons in the blue fluid of their screens.

All across America, yogis rise and fall, shifting from asana to asana, a flight of birds, a school of fish, these sea plants, slow and fluid as underwater ballet, tendrils curling up and out, dreadlocks poking like tarantulas from their crowns. Nothing like India, where the stern yogi barks out asanas as if bored, no props, no blocks, no choices, no options, no accommodations for special feelings or unique moods.

I hear the Dalai Lama warmly chuckling, the American yogis have a ways to go, their moans and sighs so long and overdrawn, poses birthing long, laborious vowels announcing the depths of their stress. The countless choices of poses given, riddled with *You decide, it's up to you*, their warrior pose a bit too self-righteous, Ujjayi breathing more like steamboats than the vastness of ocean, Savasanas like islands, each psyche shipwrecked by its own perceived uniqueness.

Over and over they need to be reminded—in one year 98 percent of their atoms will exchange for new ones. Thoughts rise and fall like meteorites, fireballs aglow with a feisty energy that eventually fizzles and withers. With each outbreath, the entire cosmos released from the body's cage.

Monsoon Clouds

DARJEELING, WEST BENGAL, INDIA

We walk up the ratty, muddy roads, pockmarked with monsoon holes. The ground slimy, scabbed with cement chunks, candy wrappers, and dog shit. Tenzin stops to buy a Coke from one of the dark stalls like catacombs alongside the streets, ducking under hanging legs of yak meat, poking around bowls of spices, bangles, biscuits, fabrics, cheap Chinese sunglasses. Open fires and ragged barking dogs. I wait outside, suddenly alone, awkward, without the comfort of Tenzin, or He Who Makes Me Legit in This Town.

At the hospital, we climb up the dark, creaky stairs dodging the limbs of ancient health care apparatuses to a room packed with wheezing elderly, some with oxygen masks, eye bandages, bubbling IVs. Tenzin's father, Lendhup, lies in a squeaky 1950s-type bed, face puffed up, his entire family packed around him, one of them a famous Everest Sherpa climber who greets me with ease as if he knows my kind, smiling as he points to my North Face jacket.

Tenzin empties his father's catheter bag nonchalantly into a bucket and dumps it out the window. Much laughter about whether a stray dog got hit. Mingma is wrapped around their mother, absent-mindedly stroking her hair as she feverishly works the prayer beads. In between jokes, coughs, and sips of canteen tea, mantras get slurped in and out with the breath. Mingma turns suddenly, leaving her infant open mouthed, and stunned, exposing her glistening dark nipple.

Though I should love it here, it's hard to breathe, almost suffocating, a kind of humid, muggy kinship I'm not used to. Like so many Americans, I need the night to slink back to my hotel and dry out. Tenzin worries I'll be too lonely. My nickname here at the hotel: Lone Wolf. After the waiters have gone, I come out of my den and pile leftover buffet food onto a plate, then scamper back to my room, savagely rip into the chapatis, fried rice, and saag paneer, mop up the oily drizzle on my chin.

Tenzin takes me to his home for ginger tea and biscuits and more talk, more relatives, rescued dogs, and a resident family monk. His place is five stories up, a cloud chamber tonight. We peer out into the fog, he tells me what you cannot see is Bhutan, Sikkim, Nepal, and beneath the hills of Darjeeling thousands of shacks with tiny lights.

Tonight, the cool clouds cuddle right up to the top of his balcony. Clouds, so different here, boisterous and thick, they come right into your presence, into the house, the kitchen, the bathroom, my lungs thick and padded with a misty Himalayan gauze, my skin dewy with monsoon.

At first it feels like asthma, a kind of panic, but if I let it be, there's a calm in swallowing the clouds, in not knowing where I begin and the Darjeeling mist ends.

I tell Tenzin, in Vermont I wake to see clouds already lugging their belongings elsewhere, dogged as pilgrims, their huge white covered wagons billowing in a grand migration over the mountain.

When they're gone, I'm filled with a hollowness, like when a lover turns away, pulling the warm sheets from your body, dragging the tail end of warmth over the space that divides you—moving on, their whole body leaning into the future, and you tucked in the corner watching, shivering, the chill left behind that never seems to warm, no matter how many times you swallow.

American Bardo

WINOOSKI, VERMONT (INTERVIEWING
ELDERLY BHUTANESE REFUGEES)

In the small, dark room, under the masthead of the black TV, they slept off the night shift, curled humbly around the couch. Even as they rose from the warm rivers of their sleep, there was a desire to please us.

Trying not to watch as they untangled, warm, grunting, bangled, bhindi-ed, smell of momo steam and milky sandalwood as their bodies pulled apart.

Long ago, as a child, just as I was dosed in praise, learning my ABCs of self-promotion, protecting my self-esteem, their limbs had been soaking in a warm kind of amniotic humility, each porous cell knowing its place in a karmic migration toward bent head, lowered eyes, stooped shoulders.

Nervous, we repeated our overly cheery "Namastes," hyped facial affect sent out like stretchers to cover the cultural divide. The old woman took us to a side room where her husband lay wrapped head to toe in white sheets, feet stuck up like crows. After she poked him, out slipped a puffy face, alive but weighted with excess sleep, the cheap antidote to boredom. *He sleeps to pass the time*, his wife says. While my translator talks Nepali, I wonder how many times his soul had tried to ascend out of the great American bardo, like the July 4th balloons still locked in his room, trapped by the ceiling, tap-tap-tapping their Morse code of attempted escape, now blown around by the Walmart fan his wife proudly brought in to cool us.

We say our goodbyes, step onto the chipped concrete, squinting at shards of winter light.

We haven't hardened back into our cockier selves as we weave toward the car, the street's rap pummeling, the traffic lurching and honking. Amid the thick bark of weathered selves, we try and stay low, stay tender, the warm mist of this house of souls still rising from us.

Refugee Encounters with Feelings
of a Capitalist Kind

NEPAL AND EN ROUTE TO NEW YORK

Across the aisle sits Bimal, the elderly Bhutanese man who sold me tea from his shack in a soggy camp where work is rare, people too poor for TV or iPhones, everyone sticky with desire for face-to-face interaction. Each day he clambered through thickets of greetings, jungles of curious tendrils, viscous eager stares insisting on a response.

Especially during the monsoon, when people got bored with staying inside, drama was high, feelings hung about for months, ripening, fermenting, refusing to dry.

Now, on this sterile, silent flight, bulleting toward New York, he fidgets with the remote.

It's agony to watch, like a lamb at a cold plastic teat, clumsy, awkwardly fumbling. I watch him rise, drag his smile through the aisles of passengers docked at their stations, silently feeding, searching for passengers between movies more apt to engage because all he needs is one kind exchange to take back to his seat and feast on. He hasn't learned how to point the remote like a wand until colors explode, surfing the channels of HBO, Netflix, Amazon, deciding how he wants to feel from menus of shows with limited-liability feelings that won't drench the psyche for too long, interrupt the workday, or dampen a vacation. Disposable feelings that can be taken off, stuffed like a kerchief into a sleeve once the credits roll and the plane begins its bumpy descent.

When the beverage cart reaches him, he milks the stewardess's sweet but weak emotional tug for all its worth, her smile no stronger than a twice-used teabag, her cheery banter, chirping high above him, noncommittal, casual, as she cracks the sodas open, shovels in ice, pours, repeats, her kindness glistening on her motions without slowing them down.

I watch Bimal fumble, nervous, already he knows not to take too long, or let his coil of loneliness unfurl. I worry the soda will spill, spread like shame across his lap, but how quickly Coke accommodates her frantic pace, seeping into the hollows of the ice cube skulls, and when there's no more room, or time, and the plane begins its measured descent, how efficiently the foam rises, bubbles, settles as it lands on his tray, the mist barely gracing his chin.

Happiness

Long before the most tender of feelings fled the Technocene, they tried to be obedient, to pass as normal, squishing their ineffable, doubting, gnaw-longing moods into sunny emoji molds. They squeezed themselves into chat rooms, tweets, dressed themselves in Second Life, garnished every text with silly memes, emoticons, trying to pass as pert and Happy.

Some of them tried to pass as normal, rode the subway all made up, returned home bruised and beaten.

When Apple produced the menstruation emoji, the feelings appreciated the gesture, the attempt to be inclusive, but still they felt left out, moaned late at night, lonely, unfulfilled. They called to each other across the landscapes, but amid the wild proliferation of McHappy, McSad, McAnger, McFear, they saw themselves reflected nowhere.

So the feelings left town, floating up like ghosts, leaving emoji husks to litter the landscape. Now the most endangered of them, the bruised and tattered, the hybrids and shape-shifters, float above the new world like shadows, hovering, longing for release, dying to slip back into the skin of the human race again, where they used to swell, linger, surprise, and confound. Now they drift above the highways' tight, manic currents, the megamalls, neon commercials, squinting from the billboards' glitz and bling.

All night their shadows slide across the sky, across the sweet night's skin, the fins of their gray, moody undulations rippling through the vast fluid of space. Like stingrays, they are waiting, hunting, hunting, to slip under the bruised parts of America, the dark spaces that have yet to close, the last tender fontanels of its skull.

American Skateboarders

MALMÖ, SWEDEN

More hijabed refugees than blondes, blue-collared Malmö sprawls, gray industrial bleak, shipyards hunkered down, sheepish against the North Sea's daily whippings.

My son dodges my lectures on all the grim global forces at play, the capsized dinghies, the Syrians and Iraqis clawing to shore.

He and his skateboard crew, oblivious, just want to cruise, look for ledges, lines, angles, jumps, and fly as one, scraping the streets into joyous rage, a gritty, reckless surfing, a brotherhood, an ownership, a cocky love of the carve, tilt, and lean.

Impossible not to envy their graceful streetsurf, afraid of nothing, it seems, not the cracks, ruts, gullies, benches, stairs, police. In quick high-fives, they slap their tags on stop signs, crosswalks, mailboxes, bits of anarchy spitting sparks in their wake, neon grins stoked with a confidence only American preschools breed.

Downtown, I interview a Syrian girl in black hijab, weighted with grocery bags, her tiny brother with his water-logged black eyes hiding behind her legs.

My son's crew races by, metallic thunder, steel vibrations crashing in their wake.

I wait for her awe to ignite, seduced by their energy's defiant magnetic pull.

But no part of her is enticed by this brilliant tornado, this roving cocky brotherhood—no envy, no anger, no awe, her face deadpan with settled fate, that some fly and others wait.

All day they scrape, jump, and slide off rails, ramps, stairs, then disperse, flying like hawks, scanning the city for the choicest concrete prey. Each fountain, statue, stone bench, or table an invitation, an appropriation, a democracy, a chance to play.

What do you think of this? I say. She looks down, clucks a *tsk tsk*, in cities, she says, it is best to be *wadie* (humble) around such shapes.

Late that night, dressed in black, speckled in spray paint, the boys gather, a murder of gangly crows. In their notebooks, they mimic Basquiat, Banksy, and urban hardcore, but as free as they are, they want more and more. So they sneak out to slam, bomb, and slash tags.

Later a phone call, the Swedish police, my son arrested—chased, pinned, pepper sprayed, strip searched, he sits blind in a cell for hours before being released.

The next morning I scan his mood for trauma's detritus. Is it any wonder he rises nonchalantly, the mild beatings miniscule molecules swallowed by his feisty cultural DNA, police humiliations eaten up and silenced by the great American self-esteem machine?

Remember *Circle Time*, each child's story painstakingly worshipped and adored, remember the *The Sky's the Limit* poster on his bedroom door.

Is it any wonder the next morning he is giggling and joking with his friends, roughhousing like puppies, tweaking his videos, reworking a trick, rejoining his radiant crew as they scarf down cereal and begin another day as kings?

On the flight home, we look down on grim Malmö with its tight-lipped streets, quiet and prostrate, how it just accepts a kind of bifurcated fate—while refugees lock their doors and sleep, American boys awake, spilling onto the concrete, as if the streets were begging them, *Come American boys, unfold, create, do with us what you must to feel great.*

Breathe with Me Barbie

BURLINGTON, VERMONT
(WITH SUDANESE REFUGEE GIRLS)

Every day, the girls, named after the colors of cows, pour Barbie body parts from the plastic bag, smudged makeup, ripped miniskirts, broken shoes, and botched haircuts they don't seem fazed by, strewn like a pile of prostitutes across the carpet. Because they're obsessed with Barbies, never had new ones, and I want them to like me, I leave my cranky feminist critiques aside and buy one anyway.

Breathe with Me Barbie is dressed in cozy loungewear, light blue yoga pants with little white clouds, sitting cross-legged, "Dolly" Lama style, with fifteen new joints for more realistic posing. Breathe with Me Barbie comes in black skin, too, and finally her head isn't bigger than her hips!

Press her crescent moon necklace until her chest lights up in pretty pastels, and Barbie asks, *How are YOU feeling today? Imagine your feelings are fluffy clouds. Now let's breathe in and out.*

Determined to get it right, the girls breathe hard as Darth Vader. Breathe with Me Barbie comes with a puppy, too, and four emoji clouds: Love Rainbow, Sad Rain, Happy Sunshine, and Grumpy Red. *Press one into puppy's head to express an emotion, switch them up to express a NEW feeling all your own!*

Once, I asked the girls' father, forehead scarred from his own cattle-camp days, *How are you?* He stared at me, confused, uncomfortable with this winnowing of self, stripped of tribe, seasons, and cattle, but he obliged, mumbling in Dinka, *The family is good.*

Now he laughs, watches his girls play personalized care at Mattel's Barbie Wellness camp as they mimic makeovers and pedicures, practice identifying with Barbie's sparkly pink feelings.

I want to tell them this is an odd reversal of their usual rites of passage, practiced in the United States of the tiny singular self, the psyche stripped of history, land. I want to caution the girls about the seductive Museum of Me, the cult of uniqueness fed by consumerism.

Their mother giggles as they practice. It's clear I'm the only one in the room feeling this is a Great Loss.

Back in the car, I feel ashamed for buying the girls with a cheap Barbie bribe. I'm late to Zoom yoga class, my unlimited pass buying as much union as I can pack in one month. It's a snowy COVID spring, I'm desperate for communion with anything beyond my own head. I pick at the tight buds of daffodils, pulling back their brown sheaths, loosening their casings, trying to force them to widen, expand.

I vow to myself, next time I will take the girls outside, let the sun pick at them gently, let the rain scurry across their skin like ants across peonies, until they open, widen into summer, and Barbie will be forgotten, and I will be forgiven for my trespasses, my aching ethnographic heart.

Jésus, Immaculée, and the Pig

ESSEX, VERMONT

This is where Jésus dumped Immaculée, before wandering off to tend another flock of clouds, down in the psych ward, clutching her Bible and scattered papers, preaching to the nurses. Jésus in his nursing-home bathrobe, polyester slippers, Jésus whose rings-of-Saturn halo floats passively from the fridges of all the Congolese in this quaint Vermont town. Jésus who for all practical purposes did nothing to stop her gang rape in Essex, Vermont (instead of the Congo, rape capital of the world).

Yes, Jésus gave her a tepid blessing as she left each day to work at Dunkin' Donuts, but when winter got tight and stingy, and she lost her job, snow tendrils swallowing the trailer like a great white squid, too often Jésus fell asleep in front of the TV, the heat cranked up, the trailer jungle humid, Immaculée's mind loosening enough for one fat memory to squeeze out of its cage, a frantic pig squealing in her skull. For days, the pig raced inside her head, shredding sirens of sound while Jésus did nothing from his perch on the La-Z-Boy, listless, like he'd had too much weed.

Even when the family held hands, prayed the rosary around the plastic-covered tablecloth, Jésus with his puddle-dull dopey eyes, draped like a Dalí doily over every refugee kitchen in that town, Jésus, with his tapered, yellowing fingers, could not catch the pink squealer screeching, tearing about, shattering teacups. Jésus who comes to her at night, feeling guilty, like a cat kneading the lap where it wants to settle. Jésus who circles around and around, pawing, suggesting forgiveness to the grunting white thugs, then curls up and sleeps, purring, while inside her psyche the pigs roam frantic and wild and the memory skins the moon alive.

⌗

Come, Jésus, wake up, put your Bed Bath and Beyond self to rest, give her something more than the Prodigal Son, or the social worker draped in polar fleece huddled like a wolf outside her door. Please, Jésus, rise up from your beige La-Z-Boy, put your mangy Old Testament fur on, summon the ragged dark clouds and your fake *Game of Thrones* sword. Help her pin the squirming pig down, help her finally slit the motherfucker's throat until the blood blooms relentless and warm across the floor.

Instructions for Doing Fieldwork
Tracking American Buddhists
for Interviews at the Stupa

THIMPHU, BHUTAN

Always remember, as a fellow Westerner, to them you are a predator, an irritant, an annoying reminder.

Keep a radius of at least ten feet.

Play nonchalant, even disinterested, working your peripheral vision for all it's worth.

When stalking, feign interest in a postcard of the Himalayas.

Remember it's their nature to want to distinguish themselves from you.

Beware: almost any posture will seem like hovering.

You are dealing with egos that crossed continents to flee you.

Give them a chance to take you in.

Let your presence settle in their vicinity, eventually diffusing, as does any offensive perfume. Resist every impulse to initiate conversation too early.

Once they see you are ignoring them, they will loosen.

This is the time for one long stare, a five-second zoom of the face to assess their level of approachability.

This will help you tailor your greeting to their specific needs.

They will sense you want contact. Expect nonverbal defenses to go up (exaggerated absorption in the Dharma manifested through aggressively working the prayer beads or circumambulating the stupa more briskly than usual).

Approach tentatively.

Remember their impulse is to flee. Images of their own desperate quests for meaning will pelt their brain, their own prized uniqueness suddenly seeming generic—at which point armies of neurons will rush into the frontal lobes feverishly rationalizing how they are still different, still the only *real* Western Buddhist in town.

From here, you're on your own. Good Luck!

Between Waking and Sleeping, I Look Outside as It Snows, Think about the Blunt Tool of the English Language

UNDERHILL, VERMONT

It starts like this, emptiness (*sunyata*), human consciousness like snow, refracting and reflecting, endlessly freezing and melting, each flake an infinite arctic mandala. In march the humans, like toddlers with their ABCs, smelling of Play-Doh, their generic lumps of language, bumbling and coarse, like Snow White's dwarves, each dopey word supposedly reflecting an independent entity, frozen in space and time!

This is how we take a flowing quantum soup, congeal it into solids using the blunt antennae of our limited senses. The way our language reinforces this, with its *subjects* and *predicates*, supposedly solid nouns and active verbs, masculine and feminine objects. Then the sentences, further molded fictions that stick together, misrepresent. Then whole concepts, hastily padded, packed, shaped, and thrown, before the other side can pelt them down.

Emotions rise, revenge thickens, attachment refuses to loosen its clutch, and soon humans are pummeling each other, the white mist from their raucous rumpus rising from the earth, the bodies now invisible in clouds of snow.

Crossing the Great Divide

UNDERHILL, VERMONT

Everything you or I or any other breathing thing has ever put in its mouth, nose, or soaked in
through its skin, is hand-me-down space dust that's been around for 13.8 billion years.
—James Nestor, *Breath: The New Science of a Lost Art*

I've been trying these breathing exercises lately, in the hopes that my percep-
tion of a divide between me and the outer world will disappear, a place where
the line between is more like a cobweb, gauze, or piece of old moth-eaten lace
than a solid wall.

These days I've come to think of breath as a way to cross any divide my lim-
ited human senses tell me is out there.

Tonight I'm on the back porch breathing with the lungs of the peepers and
giant maples tossed by wind. I like to think I'm sucking in the universe through
the creatures that croak and chirp in the black night. But when I get to the part
where you hold your breath until you think you'll die, screeching ambulance
cells busting down the door, I give in.

I suck in that sexy, beautiful air that is really the universe, but outlines my
own singularity again.

Amazing how my mind throws a death panic, flailing about like a drama
queen, even though it's probably quite beautiful on the other side, the gentle
pasture of perpetual union I've longed for all my life.

This Is What Sorrow Looks Like

COLCHESTER, VERMONT

Long ago, after my class on Women and War, emotional carnage was the norm.

Walking to my office, I'd offer Kleenex as the students shuffled after, faces pudgy with full-blown Sorrow. I'd slow down, out of respect for the heaviness they bore.

Sitting in my office, they took forever to dry out. Now I don't have to worry. After a film on ISIS rape, I'm good to go, no complaints of being triggered, no weepy aftermath, no need to process. It's what happens now, when I talk about war. Long ago, Sorrow was greasy, sticky, dark, bold. How it stuck to the body, oily, even toxic, like Van Gogh strokes. Now Sorrow looks like pointillist pastels, the tiny bytes, the air, the space between.

These days, just when sadness starts to congeal, sticking like the viscous mucous of frogs' padded feet, it's pecked by flocks of hungry texts, TikToks, and tweets. Oh, the internet's rabid beak.

When class ends at noon, at 12:05 I'm off to lunch, I'm texting as I walk, my nimble fingers flying from Snapchat to Iraq, Instagram to Sudan.

Peck, Peck, TikTok, TEDx, tweet, and text, behold the minced ground beneath my feet. Oh the internet's shiny beak!

Ringtone Trauma

UNDERHILL, VERMONT AND NORTHEAST
ARNHEM LAND, AUSTRALIA

I help my ninety-year-old mother select a ringtone from what Apple provides: Cosmos, Playtime, Presto, Uplift, Seaside, Crystals. It's November in Vermont, she's tucked in her fleece pajamas and gaudy First Responder necklace that tries but fails to be beautiful.

Knowing she hates her iPhone, and loneliness will up her tolerance for my anthro-speak, I tell her the Yolngu aborigines have iPhones now, their ringtones recordings of dead relatives singing the Lightning Snake Call while family responds, weaving their voices together.

I babble on, for now, her loneliness patient. I try to lure her in with thick and juicy description I haven't earned, as I've never been to Australia, only seen a film about the Yolngu.

When the great snake ancestor tastes the flush of fresh monsoonal waters, he stands spiked on his tail, spits lightning into the sky, electric webs threading across the night connecting all the clans.

I tell her, like Pavlov's dogs, ringtones prime the Yolngu to swell with love/ memory/clan-longing/ache, a feeling we have no word for in English.

I imagine Apple promoting Grief, Ancestor, Dead Person Singing, our bodies still responding with a Pavlovian surge more akin to an adrenaline spike. In the Urban Dictionary, it's called *ringtone trauma*, the anxiety triggered on hearing your phone ring.

Meanwhile, my mother chooses a ringtone called Twinkle, the slowest one we can find, part lullaby, part jovial bard, part Las Vegas, its decidedly merry pluck of strings standing firm against a bewildering world.

My mother's iPhone sits atop her kitchen table all alone.

It rings, I see her wince/grimace/sigh/groan.

There's no word yet for how my mother feels when her iPhone lights up and sings a quaint and packaged past amid the whirling Technocene she is expected to navigate.

No word for how its flashy smile of bling belittles her these days. *I hate these things*, she says, fumbling with its smallness, her arthritic fingers so swollen they hit two apps at once. I watch her huddled over her phone, confused again, her puffed white hair so thin I could blow it off like a dandelion.

She sits hunched over, part hunter-gatherer, part reluctant cyborg, her tired, old body flooded with perky Apple-induced sentiments she's not used to and never asked for. It's no wonder when it rings, she looks up at me through her cataracts, wilted, resigned, like a refugee, knowing full well she can never go home again.

Mushrooms, Jungle, Yoga

NOSARA, COSTA RICA

Tired of the scalding beach, its acidic sun, the taut, hip surfers like circus stars dancing on the backs of waves, I walk inland in search of shade and quiet and maybe a bit of death. The dusty streets, murderously hot, narrow into muddy jungle paths where ruffled mushrooms sprawl and spoil like raw meat. So bold is their dying. I want to die that way too. Every rotting cell fully engaged in the leaving, drunk with resignation.

Blackbirds on stilts hide in tree limbs and watch me pass.

Leaving the jungle, I see the main tourist road ahead, lined with hibiscus, splayed red throats retching their stamens out. I know where the road goes, to a yoga center whose entrance is exotic and stunning. Fifty stone steps to the top where Ganesh is perched, then ten more to where the stone Buddha hovers over the sleek, glistening check-in desk and its twittering skinny girls so eager to help. Then five more to the top, an ecstatic emerald pool, a white woman floating on her back like a crucifix in a stiff well-earned delirium. The juice bar loud with volcanic Kale eruptions. Here the long-legged blonde goddesses of Lululemon hold court, curled like cats into padded hammocks in their sleek black leggings.

So I scuttle back down the stairs knowing I'm not quite ready to leave the slouch and sog of the rotting jungle where nothing is tight with anything, just the humble mounds of Quasimodo moss draped everywhere. Swamp. Mangrove. Bleeding fairy fungi. Fragile dapperling. Bridal veil stinkhorn. Trooping crumble cap.

In grade school, why did no one tell us to lean down and inhale the ripe rot of our self as we sat washed and preened, stiff as soldiers at our desks, and opened our fresh notepads, the white paper cold as milk, and so earnestly began our noble wars against mortality?

Why did no one tell us to put our pencils down, that we are already gloriously dying and there's no shame in that? No, children, there's no shame in death at all.

The Choice

UNDERHILL, VERMONT   *For Viktor Frankl and my mother*

After all the chemo, she knows I trust her with my ugliness.

In the dark, I hear her labored breathing as she shuffles up the stairs to my smelly chemo nest, she proudly bearing two pints of Ben and Jerry's, her loyal, dopey Labs panting after her. She cannot hear, I cannot see, so we forgo words and dive into the luscious pink cream, me mining for nuts and chocolate, she slurping indiscriminately.

After she kneads my feet, her hands still cold from cradling her pint, she rubs them into heat before massaging my bald head, stopping here and there to feel the nub of a scab, trace the arch where an eyebrow once was.

Meanwhile, Notre Dame burns, Taliban girls limp over the border, the trees shake the crows into the wind, and still no one knows anything much except that love should save us. My head deep in the soup of her belly, her stomach growls, but I choose to laugh because I'm tired of all the medical gloom, and it was she who taught me how to stay for one second in that "space between the stimulus and the response" and in that space to choose wisely.

So when her breathing rushes over the few remaining hairs on my skull and I feel the pulse of blood as her old heart pants in its cage, my spine prickles, fearing life without her.

Just before my thoughts settle, harden, I take my one freedom, in that small space that all loyal prisoners of this world cherish. I giggle and she does too, and in that space the two of us are lifted, high above the nest, which looks so tiny now, so quaint, so hopeful.

COVID Subnivean

UNDERHILL, VERMONT

Ground frozen, mice and voles on lockdown below, still they skitter beneath, not even the fox dares to dive into the snow taut with a glassy sheath of ice. The barred owls, too, are starving, crouched near bird feeders in broad daylight.

This morning, I spot a huge one huddled in the gangly clutch of our plum tree, tucked deep into its speckled feathers. I tiptoe up. No matter how close, it doesn't budge, watching me, but lapsing into sleep, grunting as it dozes off in a dopey hunger trance.

I dangle lunch meats in front of its beak, in nearby branches. Nothing. Only the tree now with its savage flags of flesh.

When the owl flies off, a great sadness swells in its wake, so I pace the house, restless, the bodies of loved ones always just behind the slick screen. I Zoom my elderly mother, passing in and out of the frame, there, but just out of reach. She doesn't know how to enlarge her screen. *I can't see you*, I think she says, but she doesn't know her mute button is on. She's confused, fumbling with her laptop keys, lost in the maze of internet logic that makes her feel dumb. Frustrated, she claws the screen as if trapped under ice, subnivean.

I want to swoop down, clutch her with my tender hooks.

I want to crack the ice, hear her gasp, I want to help her breathe.

Don't Let Anyone Tell You Anything
Is Separate in This World

PUTNEY, VERMONT

My son sends me a poem. It goes something like this:

> The grass licking the edge of the road was almost dead. It tasted the dust
> of the road and crunched on its small rocks. The smog of the dirt hung
> like grief in the air, in other words, useful to no one. A rough worn hand
> in a dirty pocket was more useful than the grief in the air. For that is
> what was happening. A hand in the pocket of a man whose lungs were
> lined with the dust his feet and shovel kicked up.
>
> Don't let anyone tell you anything is separate in this world.
>
> The grief caused him to walk, the walk caused the dust, the dust choked,
> and spied on the depravity of its creator.
>
> That man whose hand belonged in his pocket had just dug a large
> cavernous grave for his horse, one that served him dearly. Its black coat
> once was a shine, a gleam, a piece of pride. The man could still smell the
> musk of the leather saddle, horse sweat, stench of its death.

More than the shovel that dug the grave, his hands held calluses of his whole life of hard work, each like a cherry pit in hardness and sweet affirmation.

More than the carcass of the horse, the grave swallowed the man's tiredness, his longing, his lonely ache, it gulped and gulped his crippling grief. All were taken by the mouth of the grave and its blackened dirt, the dirt that turned into the dust that choked the man as he dug and dug and dug.

Aborted Ethnographic Fieldwork

Nonparticipant Observation

NEWFOUNDLAND, COAST OF LABRADOR
(WITH PINE TREES)

I was naive. I drove from Vermont in June, from humid green fields bear paw thick, blue mountains bulging with steam, white calves, heads bobbing like toy boats. I remember the sheep bunched tight as cauliflower on the distant hills. On the farms, the bulls, silent, sleepy, were just waking up, propped up all night in their giant barns of thick bone, shifting from one pillar to another. Even the spiders hanging above them were plump as blueberries, still as planets, groggy and gentle.

So forgive me, Canada, for leaving your country so abruptly. I was arriving from a kind of Tolkien Hillshire. I was exploring topics for my dissertation, to study depression among women in trailers lit from within by soap operas that belittled their lives.

Given all I had, I figured it was the least I could do.

It was sunset in the barren tundra as I crested the hill and the arctic wind slashed its knives, my breath left me.

Row after row of pine trees standing frozen, stiff, hollow-eyed skeletons, stretched silent screams.

Old, terrified women pulled taut—electrocuted, beaten, arms thrown back toward the sea.

This vast burial ground of stripped pines, who knew no better than to trust. If this is the plight of Newfoundland's trees, I thought, imagine the psyches of its humans.

I skittered back to my car, ashamed, knowing after a year in this place, I'd never make it out alive.

War McMetaphors

UNDERHILL, VERMONT

I never bought into the cancer war metaphors in pop culture, the ones my friends used in a moment of awkwardness when they were just trying to make me feel better. I can't blame them for using the dominant metaphor of the time. But I swear I never took up one metaphor of war and aimed it at my multiplying cells. I never once resonated in agreement when someone told me to keep up the good fight and kick that cancer's ass.

I wasn't invaded by enemy cells, fought with the latest ammunition in my oncologist's armory. I didn't like the image of two opposing forces locked in a battle until one or the other loses. It seemed like a Disney kindergarten version of a clunky, dichotomous world.

As the chemo kicked in, my whole body shedding, moving from solid to liquid, the seams of my borders—gums, nails, mouth, eyes—loose and leaky. Those days are the closest I've ever been to the viscerality of impermanence, to *sunyata*, emptiness, the constant shedding, morphing, and sluffing that is the world.

People still high-five me saying how well I shot the cancer down and put it in its place. How to tell them of the impermanence like a great liberation, the self finally moving with the current of some giant, inevitable river, soggy, floating in shaggy bits downstream? There's no time for explanations like this as we pass each other at the grocery store, and more than anything, I just want to be close to my fellow humans, who try so hard in their own way to be kind to me. So I smile, wince, and join the good fight.

Technotropic

DARJEELING DISTRICT,
NEPAL-INDIA BORDER

For three days we have trekked to this tiny village on a mountain ledge, devices ziplocked into padded black bags, camera antennae tucked into themselves humbly, so as not to call attention.

We are here to spread a kind of gospel of fear, warning girls that traffickers lurk everywhere. Under the rickety bamboo shack we begin with a cautionary film. Women strain toward the screen, swatting at the incense that winds like a ghost through their vision, black eyes milking the tragic plot as the villain is caught, or the girl tries to escape, their faces bruising and flowering in swells that leave not one cell behind.

Back at camp, Sherpas sport solar chargers on their backs, slick panels gleaming iridescent as beetles in the Himalayan sun. As they cook, they rotate inch by inch, technotropic, capturing the sun's last meek rays, enough to resurrect their dead phones.

Well into the night, virtual Sherpas scale the web, their North Face tents bulging at the seams, lit with a desperate, restless light, like hundreds of captured moons.

In Darjeeling, I find my daughter, my son, tucked inside the Wi-Fi café, both of them laptop glued. Unlike the Nepalis, barely a ripple passes through their faces, and what bits rise to the surface so tiny, mere minnows that flit away into the cool amniotic blue.

How long will it take, until they greet me, their eyes dutifully fixed on mine, while underneath their cells furtively gather, at first just a few, then thousands stealthily migrating back toward their screens, and though they answer my questions, little by little their tectonic plates shift, faces masking their divided loyalty with puppets I'm suspicious of, but can't readily accuse.

In the mountains, I try and coax the Sherpas out, but once the sun sinks, they zip themselves in, deep screening, recharging, digging like moles through the World Wide Web.

Perhaps someday when humans are cyborgs and the internet juices and sluices our veins, there will be a quaint name for the days when the present moment was so narrowly perceived (limited to the body's five clumsy senses, a cluster of nearby humans, a local geographic space).

Perhaps they will look back bewildered at the grief that overcame elders like me, the day we thought the psyche had fled the present moment, our young's attention scattered like birdseed.

Perhaps they will forgive our parental doom, hummed in the key of loss, laugh at our simplicity, from their perch deep inside the web, by then a kind of dazzling planetary brain, a jeweled net refracting, reflecting the infinite in its every nodule, no single source, no single present moment, a kind of blessed impermanence everywhere rising and falling.

Mating Knot

YEI, SOUTH SUDAN

Back then, between wars, when it was safe and the Lord's Resistance Army wasn't on another child kidnapping tour, our whole family stayed out in the bush while the girls' school was built. We slept in battered tents, shooing chickens away, along with the students from the college where we taught. Between the mangos falling on our tent, the diesel generator belching on and off, the diving bats, and the eerie drums marking the death of a toddler, we couldn't sleep. So I dug into my purse of endless pharmaceuticals, found a soggy Benadryl to put an end to this god-awful day.

Hours later, still awake, adrenaline waging war against Benadryl, I snuck off in the hopes of plugging in my laptop to the generator outlet.

The competition would be steep. Students watched their laptop battery obsessively, competing for the best spot near the generator in the early morning queue. Even in the dim light of moon, you couldn't miss it, a vast T-shaped vein of electric current, mauled by the charging cords of NGO laptops and iPhones, a tangled nest of dozens of cords wrapped around each other, vying for the best spot.

I could barely look at it, so like the writhing pile of snakes we saw near the river in a mating knot, the one female with her head barely risen from the suffocating mass. When I wormed my fingers deep into the pile, I risked pushing others' cords out, but amid the hot heap, I found one spot open and pushed my cord deep into the socket, hoping it wouldn't overload. I felt sick, so violent, taking so much from that stick-thin, anemic country that kept getting pummeled with war.

Still, plugged in, I felt safe, backed up, and knew I'd finally sleep. When I got back to the tent, there was my daughter, gentle, kind child of perpetual worry and wakefulness, limp and finally asleep, her fingers white-knuckle-gripped around her iPhone, her headphones on her pillow, the tiny sounds of Harry Potter skittering like mice into the vast Sudanese bush.

Humpty Dumpty Had a Great Fall

DHARAMSALA, INDIA

(HOME OF THE TIBETAN GOVERNMENT IN EXILE)

When my daughter, Ana, was six, all wispy blonde, timid, and planet eyed, we brought her to northern India, home of the Tibetan government in exile, where the Dalai Lama was giving Losar teachings. As we wound up the gutted, looped roads of the Himalayan foothills, the air grew thinner.

Our driver kept falling asleep, so we stopped in a village for chai. A group of lepers sat by the road, all blind, covered in blotches of pale skin, dressed in ragged brown tunics, their heads swaying like seals, back and forth from the fulcrums of knobby, twisted hands and gnarled, stunted toes.

I could feel Ana look, but not look at them, trying to find something that would remind her of home. She landed on a Pepsi ad proudly tacked to the tea hut, with the smiling girl who looked like her beautiful American friend Katya. Even while she peed, the steam rising from the cold Himalayan ground, she raised her head to focus on a tattered Coca-Cola poster, and the one dusty Barbie doll straddling a fake Buddha in the hut window.

Next came the quarries, whole families squatting, smashing rocks, men in white diapers, shoulder blades sticking out like wings, children covered in dust hoisting bricks into straw baskets tied to their backs.

Above the noise of children hacking the rocks to bits, I tried to explain chattel slavery to Ana. Back then, I thought my sermons on injustice would help her digest the suffering she saw, but it was all too much, so back in the car she swan-dove into my lap and hid her face the rest of the drive.

It was December, in Dharamsala, when we finally arrived at the bus station at 3 a.m.. Two young girls with matted hair knocked on the window of our taxi, begging and coughing, holding babies with limp grapefruit-size heads.

A low buzzing murmur in the distance—already the Dalai Lama had started his marathon mantras—but Ana was too scared to leave our hotel room on the top floor. So, begrudgingly, we let her watch him on TV, even though he gently giggled to his armies of red-robed monks below.

High on her perch, she sat like a queen with her two boiled eggs, tea, and toast, the cups and spoons in perfect order. Chairs and tables stood about-face, the stern soldiers of hand sanitizer guarding the room while she carefully dug out the yolk with an ornate silver spoon, the Royal Dutch one brought from home. Not one crumb allowed to stray from her plate.

When I started to weep from sheer exhaustion, she looked at me with kindness, but detachment, my sadness a well-meaning but sloppy dog salivating on the rug, getting its drool on everything. The whole room smelled of hard-boiled egg.

I thought of Humpty Dumpty, how my Forced Global Compassion Tour had pushed her over the edge.

A friend emails, joking that I'm traumatizing her, spurring a gush of motherly shame, a pummeling of panicked *what if*s that keep my mind on lockdown.

It's true, I've never given her enough tools to handle the suffering she's seen—no heaven, no Jahannam, no bardo, no blood-soaked Catholic Church, no angels, no saints, no Bible placed fat and smug as a toad on her bedside table. Mostly she's been raised on Vermont hills, ponds, our mountain's stunning profile.

All summer I watched her in the garden, she and her brother all fists and toes, digging into heaven—soil, toads, bulbs, buds—the lure of sweet long green meadows.

But *what if, what if?*

I worry, perhaps I've raised her on too many cachectic psychological diagnoses? I think of Harry Harlow's experiments with wire monkeys, how infant monkeys cared more for a soft surrogate mother than a cold metal one with plenty of milk dripping from the tube.

what if, what if

what if the cushions I proudly pad myself with (my preachy pagan Buddhism and global poverty tours) are nothing more than wire for her?

Jack Sprat, could eat no fat, his wife could eat no lean.

what if, what if she needs more fat.

Humpty Dumpty sat on a wall, Humpty Dumpty had a great fall,

I lock the door to our balcony, muting the Dalai Lama's speech. After all is said and done, funny how I piss psychomedical when I'm really scared. I vow that back home, instead of heaven or zazen, with all the king's therapists and all the king's meds, we'll put her psyche together again.

Coming Home, I Dig around
My Pharmaceutical Bag

UNDERHILL, VERMONT

Each time we came back from South Sudan, Uganda, or India, we stumbled back into our serene, pastoral life in Vermont feeling a bit like hungover actors in a play. We deboard the plane jet-lagged, drive through humidity thick as moss, and hobble up the stone path to our overfed yellow Labs, hippos who bounce cluelessly across the lawn to meet us. The gentlest of green mountains, the sweet, round hills. Not one house in our view, only the profile of our mountain.

We come back to healthy, well-fed, organic, free-range families who home-school or tap their own maples. It looks insane to us, and we wobble around almost squinting, the perfect health of them so glaring. All the plastic, shiny newness and right angles of houses and stores, as if we are back in a manic commercial for kitchen products.

The first night home, East and West are so jazzed in my body, I stay up, manic until morning, the way I always do upon return. I pretend to sleep after we crawl into bed at 3 a.m., smelling of polluted airports, and greasy food, hearing the peepers gossip in their giant communes near the pond, the fresh white bedsheets making us want to weep with gratitude.

Most often we are too tired to even cry. How I love those days after, when we are united in this liminal ghostly energy as we scuttle around the house in our pajamas, avoiding normal humans. We leave each other alone, but let each other wilt, snarl, eat, be grumpy.

Sometimes, when the kids don't know how to handle the wired yet dead-weight delirium of jet lag, I dig around my pharmaceutical bag and give each of us a pill that finally lets our minds slow enough to sleep. We awake disoriented, thoughts slow, dark, and gluey, hoping for night again.

After about a week, the kids' minds settle more and more, but mine stays lost for a while. I come back from long walks in the woods with drooping flowers and revelations. I vow to live my life differently here. Even through the dreamy gauze of my jet-lagged lunacy, I can tell, the kids welcome going back to school, and are happy to give me a wide berth.

But I don't want them to leave me, our little house where America's bold and beautiful make no sense.

In the car, they are caught. Speeding down the road on the way to school, me feeling abandoned, I try to bait them, seeing if I can get some company in my lostness. *Remember the puppy we picked worms out of at the camp in the bush?* They nod their heads, airily, as if absent-mindedly shooing a fly, not committing to more.

With that, it's over, I make myself shut up. They have to move on, I have to let them go, and I do, loving and hating the fact that I, too, will emerge from this dark liminal pupa to the other side, confident, cocky, self-assured, fanning my brilliant American wings.

The Careful Preservation
of Child Atoms

UNDERHILL, VERMONT

My kids just left for college, and my body is full of ache and sorrow, the way it always is when they leave. When I walk into their rooms, I can smell the essence of them and I'm comforted. The incense, menthol, and spicy soil blend of my skateboarding, sweaty boy, the calla lily fresh pure white lotus of my moon-beautiful girl, with a bit of mock orange. I don't change their sheets, not for anyone who comes to visit, because I love to crawl into their beds and know that as far away as they are, they are burrowing into me, in the same subatomic way the stars, George Floyd, Charles Darwin, Virginia Woolf, and my dead father are with me here now, in bed.

I keep their doors shut, and I don't bring in any new Target-type sheets with their processed commercial poison that will drown out their smell in five minutes. I confess I've even thought of blocking the space under their doors with clothes, but then it wouldn't allow for the kind of space you need to keep the raw part of memory alive, just enough of the outer world to seep in, not enough to smother it.

Cybirds

UNDERHILL, VERMONT

I found an app that allows my texts to alert me through birdsong, another noble attempt to combine techno with spiritual.

Someday, my monk friend says, chips in the brain will cue us to breathe mindfully, will stimulate the oceanic, religious part of our brain. One nudge from the chip, and our brain will have no choice but to perceive the self as interwoven with everything.

At nine, after my father was killed, I fled to the woods when my mother became all beak and bone, the fluted song of the hermit thrush with its toppling cascade of liquid ribbons soothing me as nothing else could.

Back from my walks, I was sniffed out by my brothers, sitting glum inside our dark house, their bowls of stewed rage steaming. Wanting to hurt me as much as they were hurt by his death, they lunged at the source of my solace, told me of the true violent purpose of birdsong, *to fend off other males and mark their territory.*

That was not the first time they took what I held sacred, pinned it like a desiccated frog in Darwin's cold lab. Even now they would tell me a scan of my awe-filled brain back then would simply have shown what neurotheologists call "a photograph of God"—a deep azure (like an indigo bunting?) glowing on the left side of my cerebrum.

So when my iPhone chirps a red-winged blackbird, I'm saddened when it zaps me into fight or flight, a flux of electrons along neurons screaming about all the shit I have to do.

In the meantime, I watch my children peck at their screens with a hunger that scares me.

Hush, I tell myself. You can't go home again, and it's no use longing for the past.

Be patient, my monk friend says, as he gently pats my iPhone as if it were alive, *over time, eventually God learns how to nest anywhere.*

Mismatch Theory

A Message from a More Mindful America

Dear Ancestors,

In many ways, not much has changed. We're still here, a scrappy, dogged species, we've crawled to the top, shoveling our genes into the next generation, made possible day after day by a grand illusion (that the self is closer to wood than wave), still sporting a bulky mind evolution left us, the thuggish one (no offense), designed for hunter-gatherers, all gunshot and adrenaline.

Our bodies still encoded with a forager's DNA, instincts misfiring like bulky cannons, hissing at predators that no longer exist, the last grand fireworks of a stubborn old genome. Despite our evolved senses, our consciousness still reports a solid body in time and space.

Yes, we still walk around upright, our brains now itchy nests of random thoughts perched high above our bodies' trunks. Alas, pandemics bloom across the earth, oceans drag villages into their bellies. You'd be amazed at how quickly happiness still evaporates under the current regime.

Yes, especially in America, we are still smitten with the fiction of a singular self, but at least now we have capitalism to channel our fight or flight. We love the way adrenaline feeds productivity. To say we are restless and stressed is an understatement, but a new tool has arrived, called meditation. It's a subtle thing, a hard sell to Americans, a rebellion against natural selection and its stubborn instinctive reactions, but a tool no less game-changing than language, fire, or the wheel.

So, yes, we're still trying not to buy into the same thoughts you had when fleeing a tiger or wooly mammoth, instead we try and watch them, note their magnetic pull, the suck of their maddening orbits, say to them gently, like a lullaby, *How interesting, there now, it's time to let you go.*

The Human TechnoBody
Meets Quarantine

NEWTON'S FIRST LAW: Bodies in motion stay in motion or at rest unless acted on by an outside force.

Heading back to Vermont, on the airplane, my son memorizes Newton's Law as he studies the collision portion of his driver's ed manual. Ten more minutes of studying until he can have the padded remote, perfectly crafted to fit his hand and predict his finger's logic.

Six Wi-Fi hours later, we land, lurch forward, our bodies belted in place despite the airplane's suctioned forward thrust. When we taxi to a halt, I want to tell him that Isaac Newton didn't account for the kinds of bodies resting half a century later that buzz and hum, unmistakably technoelectric, despite being caged, reverberating furiously with old media bytes and searches we google-suck at warp speed. That in these liminal pandemic times when life is a boxed bardo, perpetua purgatoria, the thousands of channels and tweets we have surfed and snorted up until now still glow, writhe, birth, and die like embers in our nerves, sparks fireworking across synapses, making shrapnel of our calm.

I want to tell him, despite the safety belts that tell us we are solid, separate, despite the plane's elevator music cueing us like dogs to stay, stay, though we are heading into another lockdown, we will still be spinning like meteors, restless, combusting, discreetly discharging our manic atoms by pacing, crossing and uncrossing our legs, picking our nails, sanitizing our hands, chewing gum, fidgeting through purses.

And yet all of this is barely enough to calm the rabid cells inside us, the endless flocks of neurons whose murmurations still startle, dodge, dart this way and that.

Because I just want to sit and hold his hand, I resist the temptation to tell him that someday we humans will learn to leave our bodies, cells gone, gone, nowhere and everywhere, both particle and wave, that we were never really clumps to begin with, no forward or backward, no harnessing, no holding, and once we finally know this truth like angels we will never come back, never be homesick, never be held captive again.

Our Evolution Cannot Be Digitized

And how shall we survive? We don't and cannot and will never
Know.
—Hayden Carruth, "The Curtain," *Scrambled Eggs and Whiskey: Poems, 1991–1995*

I tell my students, with a smug sense of evolution's trajectory, that they are out of their league.

No one can predict.

No matter how hard Disney tries, no matter how many previews, sneak peeks, or trailers, our evolution will not include barren colonies on Mars, Land Rovers that skitter like crabs across the cosmic dust, it will not be free-streamable, it will not look like *Star Wars, Dune, ET,* or *Lord of the Flies.*

Our evolution will not appear on screensavers as a scorched, humanless earth, as underground off-world colonies or pale aliens bathed in loving light, because our evolution cannot be Disneyfied.

Our evolution will not prove Darwin right or wrong, it will not make us happy or sad, it will not be dystopic or utopic, apocalyptic or blissful, because our evolution cannot be dichotomized.

Even if it tires of the slow pace of reproduction, jettisons the body, ditching it for artificial intelligence, our evolution will stay nowhere for long.

No matter how hard Apple tries to achieve electronic immortality, the atoms of our brain scanned, our mind transferred to computers, the whole soggy cortex replaced, our thinking uploaded on artificial hardware, even if backup copies are made and we are rebooted when earth is livable, our evolution cannot be digitized.

Even if, as uploaded beings, we travel at the speed of light through silky patterns of information, even if we download ourselves into robots that bumble like dinosaurs across Mars, our evolution will never be caught or tamed.

A Brief Respite from
the Usual Perceptual Divides

After Chemo I Ski through the Vermont Woods
in Another Climate Change Storm

MOUNT MANSFIELD STATE PARK,
UNDERHILL, VERMONT

Pumped with steroids, eyes rimmed pink, mouth sores raw, I scuttle through
the ragged birch, pale, bald, lean, and hunched. The wind writhes, arches its
back, whips its tail and leaves, branches crack and moan.

I ski deeper into the wild white roaring until I'm not sure I'm human any-
more, blind with the whirling undertow of snow, more a coagulation of dying
things, so I gladly let my sheddings be taken by the wind, its giant swirling
paw batting me about until I'm dizzy with a mixing and merging, giddy with
a blurring of the usual thuggish divides, the bulky ones the ego guards like a
bone, Anthropocene brutes, the ones that lift weights each day.

Sometimes I don't want to ski home, though it's filled with such good peo-
ple. Meanwhile, the worried wonder when I'll return, so I turn around, duti-
fully, because I don't want to disappoint.

On the couch we drink warm milk, wincing as the storm hurls itself at our
house. *Apocalyptic,* someone says, *Yes,* I say, numbly, just so I can keep on
thinking how all my life I've wanted to disperse long enough for the moon or
the owl to mistake my body for a field, *Yes,* I say again, and though we think
our minds are sealed in skulls, the hair on our arms is the first to sense an on-
coming storm.

Last Week, Tied to
My Intravenous Pole

I lay slack with the others in a chemo haze, transfixed by a TV show about the Cordyceps fungus attacking its host from the inside.

All of us watched a bullet ant stumble about as if drunk, the brain the first to go, while the colony herded it away and skittered back to work.

Soon wild neon tentacles madly unfurled through its stunned corpse.

Orange sprigs and luscious pink tendrils sprouting through its furry abdomen.

Its furry thorax cracked open. Not one of us could turn away. A kind of science fiction, the male narrator said. *Not really*, I thought, my lips cracking, my purple fungal toenails lifting from their beds.

Not really, I thought, my mouth sores, like white orchids, so perfect in their blooming, my scalp's itchy welts rising like the soft caps of mushrooms, dark thoughts poking up through my brain's tired beds, imagining all the ways humans, too, possess and poison the planet's pores.

Finally, I just closed my eyes, let the Benadryl have its way with me,

I lay there tripping, remembering a video of a sea turtle, a plastic straw they thought was a worm, poking out of its nose, all the pesticides sprouting up through the earth's battered body, emerging as the sweet green sheen of a golf course, its pesticides hidden by its velvet emerald moss, so deceptively serene. Or the dazzling iridescent skyscrapers, so quick to pierce the soil and rise, so cocky in their magnificence, their silver scales glistening with victory.

It's no wonder the whole lot of us can't turn away from our own brilliance, or that gravity still keeps us humble at all.

The Trouble with Anthropocene Grammar

VERMONT

> What is description, after all, but encoded desire?
> —Mark Doty, *The Art of Description: World into Word* (2010)

When my son was barely a year and he'd poke his head up out of the crib, all warm and yeasty, hair stuck up like two soft horns, beaming brighter than a headlight in anticipation of the nip, that's when I noticed it most, a bubbling up of adjectives, a fierce cooing, rapid fire of tiny love names:

tender pink niblet, luscious little beast, waternut, love blossom.

Latin became the cheap toy I mauled at the service of my desire, *Panis bulbosa, Lactata nippiana, Pinkus chubbisimus.*

Even as a child, as I walked the woods and came across an orange-spotted newt, owl, or deer, a kind of verbal fever, a love-smitten Tourette's rose, my brain wild with metaphor, swinging from branch to branch of simile, trying to match the newt's succulence, its adorable toddler waddle across the damp black soil.

Or in June, the pink-veined pouches of the lady's slipper, both ephemeral and genital, floating toad-balloons, half scrotum, half fairy. Walking the woods, I was a sound nymph, tickling the moss with alliteration, a Swedish masseuse rubbing the mushrooms with vowels.

Now my students are learning about the ways language and grammar shape how we think and perceive. I tell them they come from a noun-heavy culture. I'd rather be from a verb-heavy one that acknowledges the vital beingness of our world. Here, we start them young at the noun factory, the naming of everything (this is a dog, this is an apple, chicken, pencil, cloud, sun). We point and point, and when they get it right, we praise! We love to separate, atomize.

We are reading about the Potawatomi language, and I can tell the students are hungry to experience nouns as verbs—to *be* a hill, to *be* red, to *be* a bay, to *be* Saturday. A hill is a noun only if grass is dead. I can tell they are intrigued. Rocks, drums, apples, fields, fire, even stories are allowed to bust down the doors of the strict *human* (alive) / *thing* (dead) dichotomy they were raised on.

Just try to be aware, I say, of how our grammar corrals us into giving a subject for every verb, so we say, "It rains" or "The light flashes" when neither one can exist without the action itself. Nor do we even note mere gradations of animacy. Lawnmowers, malls, peaches, soccer balls, iPhones, and hummingbirds are all referred to as "it."

I tell them, our grammar makes it hard for us to understand Albert Einstein's theory of relativity, but easy for us to get the linear logic of Isaac Newton's chunky objects bumping against each other. Easy for us to know when we are late to class by one minute and thirty seconds, but hard for us to smell the urine of a monkey a mile away.

I scan the classroom, one student looks crestfallen, as if she's been sentenced to a deadened world. None of them have thought about the relationship between the grammar our European ancestors passed down and the climate change that looms before them.

I want to give them hope. So I tell them, even though we are noun heavy, subject/verb dichotomous, we can still listen to the bubbling that rises inside us when we sense some*thing's* animacy (even though our language calls it *it*). Our hunter-gatherer bodies are still designed to vibrate when close to another's animacy, the frenetic hum and bubbling of the urge to describe a tulip, peach, wild rose, mountain, or fox before the next text comes in.

So perhaps for climate change we need to create space for giddy language to rise up in an intoxicating effervescence, a dizzy, almost-bewitched speaking in tongues. A space to let the endless metaphors, the vowels broken open, bowled over with awe, burst forth, landing and relanding on what you are adoring, in some guttural, visceral way. It is the doggedness of the adjectives as they crowd your mind, our species' determination to match the infinite animacy of this world, that will make it harder to destroy.

Hush, Humans

Don't tell me you didn't get a bit edgy when capitalism tossed its blond hair cockily aside, its profit settling like dandruff on earth's floor. Don't tell me you didn't squirm when giant waves of wealth rose up, hooded, lashing the beaches, then skittering away, leaving tiny husks and exoskeletons of greed (Tampons for Tweens, K-cups, tooth floss, vape coils, hair clips), all of them glistening so beautifully, mother seagulls drop them like jewels into their young's raw squawk.

You can finally let it all go, the Anthropocene, Technocene, Thermocene, Capitalocene, Coronacene, whatever it will be called. Up north, glaciers drip into Inuit trailers, bedsheets block the overeager sun. Gangs of bony polar bears roam settlements on lockdown.

What's done is done. For once, stop moving. Let yourself be still as the arctic blue.

Surely you knew something was out of balance when you looked up from your taxi, into the beehives of Marriotts, Hyatts, and Hiltons—bulging matri-archs that lodge themselves high above the composting slums, beneath them the rickshaws picking their way through piles of plastic like the praying mantis you saw on TV.

When monkeys took over the markets, stealing ripe fruit and warm infants alike, surely you wondered how long you could stay at the top of the food chain. When dusk sheepishly comes to your cities, gets swallowed by your neon blaze, when ten billion lights blanket the dark and the ego feels giddy and high, let go, right there, in that exact spot.

Soon enough a moody storm will pluck you off like dog hair from the black night's sweater. Let yourself float into the galaxy where you came from. Don't tell me you never once longed for your own oblivion. I promise it won't hurt, to let yourself fade. Oddly enough, nothing you have ever experienced under evolution's rule will ever feel this good. You only have to be ready to crouch, to be humble. I promise, nothing, no possible permutation of carbon and hydrogen we now call humans, will ever be this exhausting again.

Fontanelegy

After birth, when they finally brought my daughter back, dry, pink, and powdered in a Princess Pretty onesie, already she smelled alien, like T.J.MAXX, like Pampers, so I huddled like an ape over her tiny skull, mouth grazing across her scalp, frantically searching for her soft spot, the fontanel, its warm, pulsing cave no bigger than a dime, barely covered with a slip of furry skin.

Lips pressed against it, I felt her heartbeat's manic flutter in my throat, unfinished nerves sparking and misfiring, tiny wings of her blood pulsing. She latched on, sending me a fierce Morse code through the language of suck.

Twenty years later, an anthropologist, I roam the earth's skull with the same urgency as the day I first held her, feeling for the vulnerable spots, the cultural fontanels, the warm parts that throb, back alleys, where shapes shift, asylees huddle, girls pass like shadows between spirit and flesh, where refugees hide in comas and won't come out until it's safe, the tender places that swell between borders, where the status quo groans, the internet is sketchy, Sherpas and shamans caught between YouTube and soul loss, avatars and graveyards, iPad and axe, where globalization creeps forward, drapes thinly across a village's back.

Bless the liminal, those speaking in tongues, the dented and supple.

Bless the cartilage, the soft spots built into evolution that refuse to harden, the places on this planet with mouths hanging open, the dark fontanels that still ripple like wide-eyed ponds, the skull plates hovering like sharks.

ACKNOWLEDGMENTS

I would like to thank all of my refugee, cultural anthropology, and creative writing teachers, friends, and family who made this book possible in various obvious and subtle ways, past and present.

For all of the refugee outreach and support you provide: Africa Education and Leadership Initiative: Bridging Gender Gaps through Education, for Anita Henderlight, the dazzling force behind the Africa Education and Leadership Initiative (http://www.africaeli.org), Vermont Refugee Resettlement Program, Association of Africans Living in Vermont, Mercy Connections, Wazirgul Hashimi at Vermont Afghan Alliance, Tuipate Mubiay at Conversation Partners, Community College of Vermont, University of Vermont's Connecting Cultures, New England Survivors of Trauma and Torture. For all of the people at the Observing Minds Lab in Haifa working to bring mindfulness to refugees.

For their warm and gracious hospitality in Darjeeling and insight into sex trafficking in West Bengal, thanks to Paulzor Drukpa and Nirnay Chetri.

For Sioksian Pek Dorji for her always gracious welcomes in Bhutan.

For Buddhist teachers His Holiness the 14th Dalai Lama, Pico Iyer, Robert Thurman, Mathieu Ricard, Tara Brach, Jack Kornfield, Laughing River Yoga, Brian Tobin, Pema Chödrön, Chögyam Trungpa, Robert Wright, and David Foster Wallace (*This Is Water*) and for my dear husband, Robert Jan Lair, for his dogged and fearless optimism, big mind, and wide Buddhist perspective, always my best editor and very best friend.

For Atem Deng, Adieu, Aluel, Susu, Deborah, and Jurkuch, my South Sudanese family. For Sadig Babur, my Nuba son.

For my beloved children, Ana and Willem, for their deeply artistic souls, their love and loyalty to our home in Vermont, for laughter and kindness, and my mother, Suzanne, for all of her love, fire, and wisdom through the years. For Neera, my dear Nepali daughter.

For Bruce Weigl for his endless compassion, humor, encouragement, and epic feedback; for Peter Conners at BOA Editions for giving me a start; for Misha Cahnmann, Renato Rosaldo, Kim Gutschow, Liz Powell, Barbara Murphy, Angie Palm, Karla Van Vliet, Stephen Cramer, Tim Seibles, Brian Turner, Yusef Komunyakaa, Uwem Akpan, Dave Eggers, Laura Dickerman, Dana Walrath, Jen Gates, Carolyn Forché, David Huddle, and Michael Simms.

For Toni Messuri, Richard Does, Amy Seybolt, Ann Linde, Leslie Gibbons, Crystal L'Hote, Kathy Hanson, Rachel Inker, Trevien Stanger, Christina Root, Rai Farrelly, Jason Bagdade, John Izzi, Christine Rushforth, Roxanne Scully, Becky Hill, Vince Bolduc, Jasmine Lamb, and Chet Scerra. For Karl, Nicola, Paul, and Serena.

For Anne Brackenbury for guiding me through the submission process with such kindness and warmth. For Dean Smith, my editor at Duke University Press, for being so enthusiastic and supportive of my attempt to meld poetry, memoir, and anthropology into one.

For anthropologists, sociologists, and journalists I have admired and learned from: Philippe Bourgois, Paul Farmer, Ethan Watters, Pierre Bourdieu, Rachel Aviv, Roy Richard Grinker, Nancy Scheper-Hughes, Tanya Luhrmann, Katherine Boo, Michael Pollan, Ruth Behar, Sebastian Junger, Daniel Everett, Kevin Bales, Jill Bolte Taylor, Eliza Griswold, Kathleen Stewart, Anne Fadiman, Robert and Sarah LeVine, Nastassja Martin, Rob and Rindi Gordon, Robert Jay Lifton, Edie Turner, and Dell Hymes.

For the Society for Humanistic Anthropology for encouraging anthropologists to write from the heart.

Also thanks to the Mind and Life Institute Summer Research Fellowship, Arthur Kleinman, Byron Good, and Charles Lindholm at Harvard University; Michael Jackson and Wendy McDowell at Harvard Divinity School; Anand Pandian for inviting me to the School for Advanced Research Seminar long ago. For Christopher Merrill and Catherine Filloux for an eye-opening time in South Sudan with the University of Iowa International Writing Program.

For St. Michael's College, and my sociology/anthropology department, for giving me the width and support to be both an anthropologist and a creative writer over the years. For my students who take the work of helping and learning from refugees deeply to heart.

For my father, 1924–1975. For the land where I grew up, now live, and return over and over: the mountain, the meadows, trees, flowers, and animals of Underhill, Vermont.

✤

I would like to thank the editors of the following journals, in which these pieces have appeared, some in altered form, under different titles.

Alaska Quarterly Review: "Last Week, Tied to My Intravenous Pole"

American Poetry Review: "Patchwork Quilt for a Congolese Refugee"

Anthropologica: Journal of the Canadian Anthropological Society: "One Life to Live: Resignation Syndrome"; "Refugee Encounters with Feelings of the Capitalist Kind"; "Skateboarding, Malmö, Sweden"; "Technotropic"

Anthropology and Humanism: "American Bardo"; "Patchwork Quilt for a Congolese Refugee"

The Best American Poetry 2008: "Skull Trees, South Sudan"

Crumpled Paper Boat: Experiments in Ethnographic Writing: "On the Brilliance of Your Story"

Diode: "A Brief Respite from the Usual Divides"; "Cybirds"

Green Mountains Review: "The Choice"; "The Human TechnoBody Meets Quarantine"; "I Watch My Daughter Snort Google"

Harvard Divinity Bulletin: "After His Death, God Looks Down on a Yoga Class"; "Tulip Fever"

Harvard Review: "The Sweaty Tribe/From Heaven, Mother Theresa Looks Down on Daya Dan"

Himalaya: The Journal of the Association of Nepal and Himalayan Studies: "American Bardo"; "Himalayan Facebook Fiction"

The Hopper: "Hush, Humans"

Juxtaprose: "Field Notes—Nursing Home Fieldwork with Students"; "Psychocolonialism"

Kenyon Review: "Skull Trees"

New England Review: "Breathe with Me Barbie"; "The Fat Claw of My Heart"; "Home of Confident Children Out of Conflict"; "Mating Knot"; "Trauma, Inc."

Open: Journal of Arts and Letters: "Quarantine Dreams"; "Revised Lonely Planet Guide to Holy Men"

Peripheries: A Journal of Word and Image: "Happiness, Inc."

Plume: "What Makes Us (Not) Buddhists"

Poetry at Sangam (guest edited by Brian Turner): "The Dalai Lama and God Look Down on a Snowball Fight"; "The Dalai Lama Looks Down on a Yoga Class"; "The Dalai Lama Looks Down on Humans in the Modern West"

Prairie Schooner: "South Sudan Elegy"

Rattle: Poets Respond to the News: "After His Death, the Dalai Lama Looks Down on a Yoga Class"

River Teeth: "COVID Subnivean"

Roads Taken ("Contemporary Vermont Poetry" issue, edited by Sydney Lea and Chard Niord): "Patchwork Quilt for a Congolese Refugee"

Salmagundi: "Jésus, Immaculée, and the Pig"; "Patchwork Quilt for a Congolese Refugee"; "Refugee Christmas Eve"

Slippery Elm: "Happiness, Inc."

Vox Populi: "Breathe with Me Barbie"; "The Dalai Lama and God Look Down on a Snowball Fight"; "The Dalai Lama Looks Down on Earth"; "Happiness, Inc."; "This Is What Sorrow Looks Like"

War Literature and the Arts: "Jésus, Immaculée, and the Pig"; "Patchwork Quilt for a Congolese Refugee"; "Refugee Christmas Eve"; "South Sudan Elegy"